See for Yourself:
A Health Care Provider's Guide

*to Conducting
Internal Investigations
and Audits*

*Mark A. Srere, JD
Donna K. Thiel, JD
Aretha D. Davis, JD*

See for Yourself: A Health Care Provider's Guide to Conducting Internal Investigations and Audits is published by HCPro, Inc.

Copyright 2003 HCPro, Inc.

ISBN 1-57839-302-7

HCPro provides information resources for the healthcare industry.

HCPro is not affiliated in any way with the Joint Commission on Accreditation of Healthcare Organizations, which owns the JCAHO trademark.

Mark A. Srere, JD, Author
Donna K. Thiel, JD, Author
Aretha D. Davis, JD, Author
John Leonard, Senior Managing Editor
Jean St. Pierre, Creative Director

Mike Mirabello, Senior Graphic Artist
Matthew Sharpe, Graphic Artist
Tom Philbrook, Cover Designer
Paul Nash, Group Publisher
Suzanne Perney, Publisher

Advice given is general. Readers should consult professional counsel for specific legal, ethical, or clinical questions.

Arrangements can be made for quantity discounts.

For more information, contact:

HCPro
P.O. Box 1168
Marblehead, MA 01945
Telephone: 800/650-6787 or 781/639-1872
Fax: 781/639-2982
E-mail: customerservice@hcpro.com

Visit HCPro at its World Wide Web sites:
www.hcmarketplace.com, www.hcpro.com, **and** ***www.himinfo.com.***

07/2003
20239

Contents

Contents

Chapter Three: What to look out for—Applicable law 29

Chapter Four: Preserving attorney-client privilege and work product protection .41

Chapter Five: Employee interviews 77

Contents

Chapter Six: Disclosure of overpayments—What do you do if you find a compliance problem? 101

Chapter Seven: Responding to search warrants . . . 121

Chapter Eight: What the Sarbanes-Oxley Act means to you 145

Contents

Chapter Nine: Ethical considerations in conducting the investigation—Focus on exempt organizations 175

List of figures

About the Authors

Mark A. Srere, JD

Mark A. Srere is a partner in the Corporate Investigations and Criminal Defense practice at Morgan Lewis & Bockius in Washington, D.C. Mr. Srere counsels corporate clients on compliance issues and CCP internal investigations. He represents defendants in criminal proceedings, from grand jury appearances to trials. Mr. Srere has represented companies and individuals in health care investigations, SEC investigations, environmental investigations, Department of Transportation proceedings, and major fraud investigations, including tax fraud. In addition to his experience in white-collar criminal defense and corporate compliance, Mr. Srere has extensive experience in civil litigation both for plaintiffs and defendants in areas that range from complex toxic torts to medical malpractice and commercial litigation.

Donna K. Thiel, JD

Donna K. Thiel is a partner in the FDA/health care regulation practice at Morgan Lewis & Bockius in Washington, D.C. She focuses on regulatory issues affecting health care providers and CCP practitioners in their operations, transactions and compliance efforts. Her practice focuses on Medicare and Medicaid payment systems. Ms. Thiel represents a broad range of providers and practitioners, including hospitals, nursing homes, laboratories, rehabilitation providers, ancillary service providers and physicians.

Aretha D. Davis, JD

Aretha D. Davis was an associate in the litigation practice at Morgan Lewis & Bockius in Washington, D.C. Ms. Davis's practice focused on representing individuals and corporate clients in connection with criminal investigations and prosecutions related to numerous federal offenses, including a wide array of fraud in the pharmaceutical, health care and aviation industries. In May 2003, Ms. Davis left the firm and the practice of law to pursue a dual career in medicine and public health policy.

Introduction

The day may come for a provider when a hotline call, a routine claims review, or a whistleblower's complaint brings some bad news from the compliance front. A disgruntled employee or an anxious competitor may suggest that a provider has criminal or civil liability for its acts or omissions. Is the whistleblower correct? Has the auditor unearthed a previously unrecognized problem? These questions may force the provider to decide whether or not to undertake an internal investigation.

This book is intended as a guide for health care providers in conducting internal investigations and audits when problems with potential civil or criminal consequences are discovered. The book begins with a discussion of how to inform and educate the decision-maker as to the potential need to conduct an internal investigation in certain circumstances. Next, it discusses the triggers that might justify conducting an internal investigation, along with suggested initial planning and organizational steps to be taken, e.g., the scope of the investigation, identification of the persons to conduct it, and the legal issues involved. It then provides an overview of the federal civil and criminal laws that apply in prosecutions of health care fraud and abuse cases and identification of the agencies and personnel that pursue such prosecutions.

The remaining chapters focus on specific legal issues that may arise in the context of conducting internal investigations. Chapter Four discusses the necessity to preserve the attorney-client privilege and work product protection during the course of an investigation. Chapter Five provides pointers on interviewing employees during the fact-finding process, while Chapter Six discusses disclosure considerations arising from discovery of an overpayment compliance problem. And Chapter Seven, dealing with search warrants, tells you what to do when law enforcement agents appear on your doorstep. This chapter also includes a helpful checklist for handling search warrants.

Chapter Eight discusses the extensive corporate disclosure and ethics provisions of the Sarbanes-Oxley Act of 2002. As well as the implementing regulations issued by the Securities and Exchange Commission, and includes practical recommendations for complying with that law. The final chapter provides an overview of ethical considerations in conducting internal investigations, focusing on exempt organizations.

We hope that this guide will serve as a useful tool to ensure that your company can promptly respond to problems that may raise significant criminal or civil liability.

Informing and educating the decision-maker

In many companies, it is the compliance officer who first becomes aware of a potential compliance problem that could lead to civil or criminal liability. However, he or she is unlikely to decide whether to conduct an internal investigation. It is likely that the board of directors or other governing entity will have the ultimate authority to make that decision. One of the primary tasks for the compliance officer, therefore, is to provide the governing entity with enough information to decide whether to undertake an internal investigation.

Informing the decision-maker

An initial presentation to decision-makers will begin with an explanation of why the provider may need to engage in an internal investigation.

Next, there should be an explanation of how the internal investigation will be conducted, including such elements as scope, preserving attorney-client privilege and work product protection, and possible steps to be taken at the conclusion of an investigation.

Potentially reluctant decision-makers should be persuaded that an internal investigation would be not only a worthwhile investment, but also may be the most effective way to demonstrate leadership in corporate compliance.

The threshold issue: Why consider an internal investigation?

The initial task of the compliance officer will be to educate the decision-makers about the nature of the potential compliance problem, providing enough information to enable them to make the appropriate decision. It is important not to sensationalize the known facts or to speculate about the consequences before the investigation begins.

Because all the facts will not be known, the compliance officer may be in the uncomfortable position of repeating allegations or assertions made by someone often perceived as not "on the same side" as the provider, giving rise to scepticism. That scepticism leads naturally to a discussion of the benefits of further information-gathering. By engaging in a formal internal investigation, the provider need not speculate about the scope of real or suspected problems, and the provider can avoid reliance on rumors, supposition, or appearances. If no problem is revealed, the provider may be able to defuse a volatile situation with a potential whistleblower or a government investigator.

If there truly is a problem, the investigation will unearth and terminate illegal, improper, or reckless conduct. Once the facts are known, the provider can undertake appropriate remedial actions to ensure that mistakes are not ongoing or repeated.

The compliance officer may point to the company's compliance program. In most compliance programs, and in particular, those based on published compliance program guidance issued by the Department of Health and Human

Services (HHS) Office of Inspector General (OIG), providers commit to fact-finding upon receiving "reasonable indications of suspected non-compliance."

> [I]t is important that the chief compliance officer or other management officials initiate prompt steps to investigate the conduct in question to determine whether a material violation of applicable law or the requirements of the compliance program has occurred, and if so, take steps to correct the problem.... Records of the investigation should contain documentation of the alleged violation, a description of the investigative process, copies of interview notes and key documents, a log of the witnesses interviewed and the documents reviewed, the results of the investigation, (e.g., any disciplinary action taken) and the corrective action implemented.[1]

As former Inspector General June Gibbs Brown observed in her March 9, 2000 "Open Letter To Health Care Providers":

> The best evidence that a provider's compliance program is operating effectively occurs when the provider, through its compliance program, identifies problematic conduct, takes appropriate steps to remedy the conduct and prevent it from recurring, and makes a full and timely disclosure of the misconduct to appropriate authorities.

Safeguards in the internal investigations process

The OIG's "Open Letter" clearly links internal investigations, self-disclosures, and compliance. The tricky aspect of an internal investigation is that it may trigger the duty to self-disclose overpayments, inaccurate billing, or other compliance problems. Before setting an internal investigation in motion, the provider must consider the consequences of digging into the suspected problem. Providers must carefully balance the benefits of acquiring information against the likelihood of disclosure of both the fact of the investigation and its fruits during any litigation or government investigation.

Performed without adequate care and proper preparation, the internal audit may create a roadmap for investigators or private plaintiffs seeking to establish the provider's liability. Accordingly, the initial presentation to the decision-makers must include an explanation of the proper conduct of the internal investigation, and the safeguards to be put in place before any investigation is taken. It is important, even at this early phase, to use due care to preserve attorney-client confidentiality and to ensure that all future communication—internal or external—about the issues identified and the conduct of any fact-finding be coordinated through a single individual or task force. See Chapter Four, "Preserving attorney-client privilege and work product protection."

Providers should be firmly discouraged from initiating non-privileged fact-gathering in the form of demands for explanations, information, or opinions from employees or consultants who are not included within the attorney-client privilege. These reports would likely not be privileged, and in addition, these activities could implicate criminal statutes on witness tampering and obstruction of justice.[2] It is also important that those in charge, and those doing any investigation, discourage the natural inclination of loyal employees to "pretty up" the picture. Providers risk obstruction of justice charges if inappropriate actions are taken to cover up alleged wrongdoing.[3] Of course, a provider should act with appropriate haste to halt a potentially unlawful practice, thereby limiting potential damages and demonstrating that it acted as a responsible provider. However, it is not wise for managers to act autonomously to terminate employees or extricate the company from problem arrangements until such actions are recommended by counsel.

The reluctant decision-maker

After discussing the complex issues involved, it is no surprise that many compliance officers have trouble convincing decision-makers that the internal investigation is the appropriate response to bad news. In light of the potential costs and concerns that may be triggered, decision-makers may be tempted to declare the problem "in the past," or to chalk it up to isolated bad judgment in the field, or by misguided,but departed employees.

However initially comforting, such tactics may have far-reaching negative effects within the company. Valued employees may view management as unresponsive and seek redress of their concerns outside the company. Hotline calls and whistleblower lawsuits may result. Managers and other professionals may depart the company when blame is assigned, but the true cause of a problem is not determined.

Equally important, such tactics can have dramatic effects on attitudes of regulators and enforcement agencies, who will evaluate the provider's attitude toward compliance and its reaction to notice that it may have a fraud problem. Failure to take reasonable steps to eliminate a known problem can be evidence of a "knowing" violation. The provider who continues a practice when the provider has "notice" that it is a problem may be accused of willful ignorance. A provider cannot argue that a mistake is inadvertent if it ignores warning signals or overt advice to the contrary.

This is not to suggest that a provider must conduct an internal investigation or risk prosecution. Reasonable minds can differ on the advisability of the internal review. However, where the compliance officer believes strongly that an internal investigation is the appropriate course of action, he or she may need to become the advocate for the corporation's long-term interests.

If decision-makers still question the value or advisability of conducting an internal investigation, the following elements may help to persuade them that an internal investigation is not only a worthwhile investment, but is also the right course of action in many circumstances.

The letter of the law

Decision-makers who hesitate to engage in an internal investigation may ask

whether a complaint has any validity. They may assert that the compliance officer is too conservative or overly concerned about technical errors and other
minutiae. They may suggest that the interpretation offered by the compliance
officer or other complaining party is simply incorrect.

Support for the compliance officer's view may be found in the "letter of the
law." That is, it may be helpful to provide decision-makers with copies of the
relevant provisions of the False Claims Act (FCA) or Social Security Act (SSA)
that are at issue. Although many decision-makers may be generally familiar
with certain federal health care laws, few will have taken the time to read and
understand the statute or the regulations that may be at issue.

Legal authorities that the government will cite in this situation are not limited
to the formally promulgated laws and regulations. When attempting to demonstrate knowledge or reckless disregard, informal legal guidance, such as
fraud alerts, advisory opinions, manual provisions, or other interpretive guidance, may form the basis of concern about a provider's practices. Because
these often describe technical billing or coding requirements, providing these
source materials may also be useful.

Legislative or regulatory history

An allegation of wrongdoing may involve a new or untested area of the law. It
is often the case that the final version of a law or regulation does not resolve
a controversy or offer a clear interpretation of a statutory provision. In that
instance, the compliance officer may seek to look deeper into the history of
the relevant provision.

Particularly helpful in that regard are the preambles to proposed and final regulations in the *Federal Register*. These explanations often give significant insights into the position held by the HHS Centers for Medicare and Medicaid
Services (CMS). For example, the preamble to the Stark law and safe harbor
regulations offer examples and illustrations of the law's impact. Similarly, regu-

lations that are proposed, but never adopted, can also offer insights into CMS interpretations. For example, one proposed regulation would have led to the adoption of a bright line standard of when a provider qualifies for the exception to the related party rule. The proposed was never adopted in final form because of the problems associated with a bright line standard.

Opinions of experts

A compliance officer is often unable to be an expert on all operations that may create compliance risk. Moreover, it may be uncomfortable for the compliance officer as an insider to point out the errors or wrongdoings of colleagues and friends. Accordingly, an outside source may be brought in to review the compliance issue and to confirm or eliminate the cause of concern. In all instances, consultants and experts should be working under attorney-client privilege to ensure that their work product is protected.

Often overlooked as sources of expert advice are the employees at CMS and its regional offices and fiscal intermediaries. CMS may have a position or interpretation on an issue of which the provider or the complaining party is unaware. The provider can contact CMS to learn which interpretation of a controversial provision is correct. Outside counsel may even seek interpretive guidance from CMS on an anonymous basis. Although the provider may ultimately challenge the interpretation or guidance offered, the input from CMS will be helpful in judging the possible reaction of the intermediary, CMS itself, or an enforcement authority.

Citing precedents

It is not uncommon to hear "everyone does it" when a billing practice or kickback scheme is challenged. It may be helpful to show decision-makers that some people who once did it that way were penalized. To convince a sceptical decision-maker of the significance of technical compliance, a review of enforcement precedents might be useful.

The OIG Web site (*www.oig.hhs.gov/fraud/enforcement*) includes thumbnail descriptions of criminal and civil enforcement actions, and the penalties imposed. These are reported by provider and supplier type, so relevant precedents may be readily available.

Minimizing risk

While no provider relishes the prospect of a self-disclosure, the internal investigation may also enable the provider to self-disclose an overpayment, or a billing problem, before it becomes the subject of an investigation.[4] The OIG claims to treat self-disclosing providers favorably.[5]

The consequences of the alternative

The first thing you should point out is that the past years have seen a dramatic change in the government's attitude toward prosecuting health care corporations for white-collar crime offenses. Recently, there have been large and well-publicized health care fraud settlements, including the following:

• Fresenius Medical Care's $486 million settlement in January 2000
• Columbia/HCA's $840 million settlement in December 2001 and its $1.3 billion settlement in June 2003 (check OIG)
• TAP Pharmaceutical's $875 million settlement in December 2001
• Pfizer's $49 million settlement in October 2002
• Bayer's $257 million settlement in December 2002

In fiscal year 2002, the OIG's enforcement efforts resulted in 517 criminal convictions, 236 successful civil actions, and the opening of 1,654 new civil and criminal cases.[6] These settlements and the OIG's recent semiannual report confirm that the pursuit of corporations involved in the health care industry for civil and criminal prosecution is a primary goal of the Justice Department. Health care companies cannot afford to underestimate the intensity of the government's enforcement approach.

As noted above, it is important not to sensationalize the known facts or to speculate about the consequences if allegations are shown to be true, before an investigation begins.

However, a decision-maker's analysis of the risks of a particular practice or payment may underestimate the impact of a negative outcome. For example, the temptation may be to characterize a physician upcoding issue as an over-payment, suggesting that the only impact of a billing error is the financial oblig-ation to repay the excess. But while a simple overpayment might be the result of an audit of physician upcoding, there could be a more devastating conse-quence if a provider is found to have knowingly submitted upcoded claims. Several of the potential consequences include the following:

Show me the money

Under federal civil monetary penalty laws, violators may be fined up to $10,000 for each false claim and three times the amount claimed for each item of service. Thus, a provider could be presented with the following demands presented in the chart below, even in a relatively small matter. If the investigation covers several years, the fines become astronomical.

FIGURE 1.1

ACTUAL DAMAGES AND TOTAL DEMAND UNDER CIVIL MONETARY PENALTY LAWS

Actual Damages	Penalties (3x actual)	Fines ($10,000 per claim)	Total Demand
$200,000	$600,000	200 claims x $10,000 = $2 million	$2.6 million
$1 Million	$3 million	2000 claims x $10,000 = $20 million	$23 million

Where the actual damages are determined through the use of a statistical sample developed using Medicare's RAT-STATS audit software, the actual overpayment can be significantly increased pursuant to a statistical extrapolation.

Personal freedom

The SSA and the FCA have penalty provisions that include jail sentences, as well as fines. Often providers do not feel vulnerable to those criminal sanctions because they believe they did not intentionally violate the law.[7] Intent, however, is difficult to establish from direct evidence, and court cases have held that it may be inferred from facts and circumstances. That makes intent an issue for a jury.

One defense against the inference that the parties intended to violate the law is a functioning and well-designed compliance plan. Evidence of the provider's commitment to that compliance plan may be an effective way to refute the notion that a mistake in billing, for example, was the result of intentional overbilling. On the other hand, failure to follow a compliance plan, including provisions specifying when the provider must investigate alleged wrongdoing, could be devastating to the defense.

It should also be noted that guilty pleas can be devastating to both the owners and the affiliates of the organization that pleads to a criminal offense.

Exclusion

One of the potential penalties that may be imposed for knowing violations is the exclusion sanction under the SSA. The effect of an exclusion is that the excluded entity or individual is barred from receiving any payments from Medicare or from any other federal health care program.

Exclusion is mandatory where a criminal violation is involved. Permissive exclusions may be imposed where there is a finding that the provider or an individual committed any one of a list of prohibited acts, including filing excessive claims, claims for unnecessary services, failure to furnish medically necessary services, and for kickback bribes and rebates. A potentially devastating provision permits the OIG to exclude entities owned or controlled by a sanctioned individual, and to exclude individuals with ownership in sanctioned entities. Where the exclusion is permissive, the OIG has discretion on whether to seek exclusion. A provider's reaction to notice of potential problems, including an appropriate investigation into potential wrongful acts, may be significant in the OIG's decision whether to seek an exclusion, and may be relevant if the OIG's decision to exclude is appealed by the provider.

When an investigation is declined

Ultimately, a compliance officer may not be able to convince decision-makers that an internal investigation will be authorized. What then?

First, the compliance officer may seek to conduct a more limited review. It may be appropriate to seek approval for a sample or probe audit to learn more about alleged issues.

Second, the compliance officer will certainly need to address any overpayments revealed.

Third, the compliance officer may consider implementing new policies and procedures, and training should be conducted.

Fourth, the compliance officer should know his or her obligations under Sarbanes-Oxley to report problems involving publicly funded companies.

Fifth, in association with counsel, the compliance officer should document his or her efforts to bring the provider into compliance.

If the internal investigation is authorized, the following chapters will discuss the issues that are likely to be confronted. These chapters will provide some potential pointers in conducting such an investigation.

---

1   63 Fed. Reg. 8987, 8997, February 23, 1998.

2   There is a federal provision expressly prohibiting obstruction of criminal investigations of health care offenses and a specific prohibition on obstruction of federal audits. See 18 U.S.C. § 1516. Significantly, federal obstruction statutes apply to administrative investigations before federal agencies, not just criminal proceedings. See 18 U.S.C. § 1505. For a further discussion, see Chapter 3, "What to look out for—applicable law."

3   See 18 U.S.C. § 1518.

4   CMS proposed a rule, making the disclosure of "known" overpayments mandatory. Follow-up on the proposed rule would require providers that have "identified" a Medicare overpayment to return the money within 60 days. The proposed rule also requires the provider to present a written explanation of the reason for the overpayment. Proposed Rule, 67 FR 3662, Jan. 25, 2003. CMS says this proposed rule would simply memorialize the longstanding responsibility for providers, suppliers, individuals, and other entities to report overpayments, and simply establishes the time frame and process for making those reports. The regulation has not been published in final form.

5   To assess its compliance initiatives, the OIG performed an informal survey on the results of its corporate integrity agreement (CIA) negotiations. The OIG reports that favorable modifications occur in CIA negotiations with providers that have compliance programs, and that self-disclose misconduct to the government. When a CIA was necessary and an entity exhibited a comprehensive compliance program, OIG found that the time period for a CIA was reduced from five to three years. OIG Informal Review, May 23, 2001, CCH Medicare and Medicaid Guide, ¶50,558.

6   See OIG press release, "OIG Saves Taxpayers Record $21 Billion" (December 11, 2002). www.oig.hhs.gov/reading/semiannual.html

7   Several recent cases, however, have resulted in jail sentences for physicians and executives.

Identifying triggers and organizing the initial investigation

Introduction

Corporations have long been held accountable for crimes their employees committed during the employees' course of employment. This doctrine of *respondeat superior* extends even to circumstances in which the employee acts *contrary* to company policy. More recent trends in corporate liability, however, include applying the concept of "willful blindness" to a corporation's actions. Under this concept, a defendant can be found guilty if that defendant acted "with a conscious purpose to avoid learning the truth." In the corporate context, this standard allows the government to prove specific intent by pointing to "some flagrant organizational indifference" or corporate culture of violating company policy, the law, or both. In addition, and perhaps more significant, prosecutors can rely on the "collective knowledge" doctrine to prove specific intent by aggregating the knowledge of individual corporate employees to demonstrate corporate knowledge—even if no single employee had all the requisite pieces of knowledge.

In 1991, the United States Sentencing Commission helped enable corporations to avoid harsh penalties if they were convicted for the acts of their employees.

The guidelines for corporations focused on corporate compliance programs as the key to mitigating punishment. Those guidelines set forth specific attributes of a successful compliance program. Within a relatively short time, compliance programs became almost mandatory for large public companies. In fact, in the context of the duty of care owed by a director to a corporation, the Delaware Chancery Court, in 1996, emphasized the importance for directors to ensure that the corporation has an effective compliance program. See *In re Caremark Int'l Inc., Derivative Litig.*, 698 A.2d 959 (Del. Ch. 1996).

Given the ease with which prosecutors can attach criminal liability to a corporation for the acts of its employees, corporations must take an active role in preventing and detecting wrongdoing. Internal investigations are a basic tool that corporations use to ensure that the compliance program and a corporation's self-policing mechanism are working.

When deciding whether to conduct an internal investigation, senior management should consider the extent to which the company is regulated by the government, the level of seriousness of the allegations of misconduct, the likelihood that the allegations will be substantiated, and the likelihood of a government investigation. After a decision is made to conduct an internal investigation, a company should give careful thought to the planning and organization of the investigation. Several preliminary determinations need to be made before the investigation starts. The company needs to assess the legal and factual issues related to the investigation, its civil and criminal exposure, what documents need to be reviewed, and who needs to be interviewed. An investigation team must be assembled and agreement reached regarding the scope of the investigation.

All internal investigations, no matter how well crafted and conducted, will cause some disruption to a company's daily operations. This disruption can be minimized if a company's general counsel or compliance officer has an appreciation of the investigative process and is adequately prepared to conduct the investigation in the most efficient manner. This chapter discusses the various events that can trigger an internal investigation. It then outlines the important considerations in organizing the overall investigation.

Triggers for an internal investigation

Historically, companies generally initiated internal investigations only upon learning that they were the subject of a government probe. In today's current enforcement environment, such laxity is unlikely to be tolerated by government prosecutors. Health care companies, even nonprofit entities, are not immune to internal misconduct. Companies, especially in light of the Sarbanes-Oxley Act of 2002, must be more aggressive and initiate internal investigations to discharge their duty to prevent and detect wrongdoing.

A health care company may receive allegations of corporate wrongdoing from several different sources—employees, customers, competitors, auditors, a whistleblower, or the government. Common sense and good business judgment usually dictate the initiation of an internal investigation in situations where it appears that a problem exists that may serve as the basis for civil or criminal liability, even if no third parties or governmental entities are involved. Companies that are subject to a corporate integrity agreement (CIA) may have no choice but to conduct an internal investigation. Conducting an internal investigation in these circumstances is not only in the company's self-interest, but provides the company with an opportunity to be proactive, rather than to act defensively.

The importance of avoiding a corporate indictment militates in favor of initiating an internal investigation whenever a credible potential exists for criminal or civil liability. The government may decline prosecution of a company that can demonstrate its intolerance of corporate wrongdoing through: 1) an effective corporate compliance program; 2) the appropriate investigatory response to allegations of misconduct; and 3) appropriate disciplinary measures. If the company is prosecuted and found guilty, its demonstrated commitment to compliance and being a good corporate citizen can result in significant mitigation of its criminal fine under the United States Sentencing Guidelines.

The different triggers for internal investigations are discussed below. In each of these situations, a health care company must gather the requisite facts to develop an appropriate response and to justify its subsequent actions, including whether to initiate a full internal investigation, to turn the problem over to the human resources department, or to consider the matter closed.

Employee complaints

Employees are often the source of "tips" regarding compliance issues. A problem could come to light through a company's normal lines of reporting, an exit interview, or the compliance officer. It may also come to a company's attention through an anonymous call to its compliance hotline. A good compliance plan will offer some sort of confidential reporting mechanism. Public companies (as further discussed in Chapter Eight) are required by Sarbanes-Oxley to establish and implement policies and procedures that make anonymous reports of corporate wrongdoing. Possible anonymous calls give employees more freedom to report without fear of adverse employment action.

Not all employee complaints warrant a full-blown internal investigation. The compliance department should be able to sift through employee complaints to determine which ones may merit consultation with in-house counsel to see if an internal investigation is warranted. Some considerations in making such a determination include: whether the allegation involves the company's compliance (or lack thereof) with government statutes or regulations; the detail contained in the allegation; the involvement of outside parties; the seriousness of the allegation; and whether the allegation relates solely to human resources issues.[1]

A health care company is well advised to strongly consider initiating an internal investigation based on credible employee complaints, and not let the decision to conduct the investigation turn on the likelihood of a government investigation. An internal investigation based on credible allegations will then confirm or refute the allegations made by the employee.

Internal audits and surveys

Health care companies should actively self-monitor for noncompliant activity. A periodic company audit or survey may reveal significant omissions or discrepancies that could result in civil or criminal liability. If the audits or surveys are conducted pursuant to a court-mandated compliance program or CIA, the company may be required to self-disclose the problem within a certain time frame.

Companies must resist the temptation to believe that the anomalies or inconsistencies that were uncovered by an internal audit or survey are inconsequential and will never become public. An internal investigation should be conducted to determine the magnitude of the problem if the internal audit or survey findings suggest potentially serious wrongdoing. The internal investigation can then clarify whether the company is a victim of employee wrongdoing or possibly responsible for the unlawful conduct. Knowing the company's status will assist its counsel in avoiding government prosecution or alert the company to areas where it may be susceptible to abuse by third parties or employees.

The key question when an internal audit uncovers a potential problem is whether to place the initial investigation under the attorney-client privilege and apply attorney work product protection to it. Most companies' routine audit and compliance programs are not subject to these protections. Many routine problems are handled, appropriately so, through the normal audit process. Yet, if the audit reveals a problem that is sure to interest the government in a potential enforcement action, the compliance officer should consult with counsel to determine if a privileged internal investigation should be initiated. In most cases, if such an investigation is initiated, then the routine audit inquiry into those particular facts should be ended.

Civil suits and qui tam *relator actions*

Some companies first learn of corporate wrongdoing only after being served with a civil complaint by a third party such as a supplier or competitor. The existence of a private lawsuit, such as a contract dispute or tort action, strongly favors the commencement of an internal investigation so that the company can defend itself in the private action. An internal investigation in these circumstances will, help predict the development of the plaintiff's case, identify weaknesses in that case and uncover impeachment material against potential adverse witnesses. Indeed, it may be part and parcel of the defense of the civil case.

The False Claims Act, 31 U.S.C. §§ 3729-33, contains provisions that allow disgruntled employees, competitors and third parties to bring suits on behalf of the government as *qui tam* relators or whistleblowers. Even the employee who committed the acts that formed the basis for the *qui tam* action can be the *qui tam* relator. The government may opt to intervene and assume control of the case. The relator may also pursue the matter if the government elects not to intervene. Courts generally view *qui tam* cases in which the government declined to intervene with healthy skepticism.

The company may not actually see the *qui tam* complaint for some time because it may be filed "under seal," meaning it is not public information. Even in these circumstances, in-house counsel must try to find as much information as possible about the complaint so the company can defend itself.

Internal investigations can play an important role in convincing the government not to intervene in an action. Internal investigation findings can highlight legal weaknesses in the action and undermine the veracity of the action's allegations. A company may also be able to convince the government that the alleged conduct was an aberration, not a systemic problem, with evidence from the investigation.

Government audits, reports, inspections and inquiries

Government audits, reports, inspections and inquiries may reveal questionable business practices of a business unit or group of employees. In those circumstances, the company should initiate an internal investigation to determine the scope and seriousness of the problematic conduct. Once the facts are known, the company can develop the most appropriate strategy in dealing with the government. There is little doubt that if the questionable conduct came to light via a government audit, report, inspection or inquiry, the company will have to be prepared to respond to the government follow-up.

Subpoenas and search warrants

A health care company may learn of allegations of wrongdoing only after employees are approached by federal investigators or after being served with an administrative or grand jury subpoena or, by the worst case, the execution of a search warrant. If the government has chosen this route, the prosecutor generally has a belief that some serious violation has occurred and a criminal prosecution is likely. In these situations, a company has no choice but to conduct an internal investigation. The investigation should, at a minimum, mirror the government's investigation. The information gathered from the internal investigation can provide senior management with a realistic understanding of the company's civil or criminal exposure and an appreciation of the government's view of the case. This knowledge will place the company in a better position when negotiating with the government and may support the company's contention that the unlawful conduct was an aberration that was missed by an otherwise effective corporate compliance program.

Investigation strategy and scope

If the facts warrant initiating an internal investigation, the company must first carefully consider the legal and business implications of the investigation and develop an investigation strategy and plan. Although no two investigations are alike, certain basic investigating principles are applicable to all investigations. At the outset, in-house and outside counsel must evaluate the investigation's needs and objectives when developing short-term and long-term investigation plans. Steps must be taken to ensure that the investigation will be covered by the attorney-client and work product protections.[2] Once the planning stages of the investigation are over, the company's attention can then be directed to its investigative activities and then remediation, including the development of new compliance policies and procedures.

Determining the scope of the internal investigation

The scope of a company's internal investigation turns heavily on the factual circumstances that gave rise to the investigation. Certain fact patterns dictate the casting of a broad net. Other situations call for an internal investigation that is rather limited in scope, although a company should be prepared to expand the scope of the investigation if pervasive and broad-based corporate misconduct is uncovered.

In determining the scope of any internal investigation, one of the key questions is this: What kinds of issues does it raise? Health care companies may wish to develop lists of various issues that would trigger consultation with in-house counsel to determine whether to conduct an internal investigation. Issues that involve violation of health care statutes and regulations, such as submissions of fraudulent billing, false claims, upcoding, kickbacks and overpayments, should almost certainly be discussed with in-house or outside counsel. Due to the potential for government involvement, those investigations tend to be broader in scope. Issues involving patient care, including allegations of abuse or neglect, may also give rise to a broad investigation because of the potential damage to the company. Internal problems that do not involve third parties, such as embezzlement or theft of the company's property, can often be dealt with a very limited and focused investigation. These issues can often be resolved without resort to third parties.

How the problem arose may also dictate the scope of the response. If the government has already started to investigate the company, either informally or through the grand jury process, the internal investigation should shadow the government's investigation. For this to occur, the company must learn the subject of the government's investigation. This can be done in several ways. First, the company should interview any employee who has been contacted by government investigators to discover the subject areas of the government's interest. The company, through counsel, should contact the lead person in the government's investigation, whether it is an OIG agent or an Assistant United States Attorney. It is important that this contact be made through counsel familiar with government investigations so that appropriate questions can be asked. The company should further anticipate the government's moves by interviewing key employees and reviewing important documents before the government does.

In situations where an investigation is prompted by an anonymous employee complaint, internal auditor findings, or some other non-governmental or non-litigation related source, the investigation can be more limited, at least initially. It should carefully review the specific allegations to determine the facts. Unfortunately, many times such allegations are vague, and the investigation may have to be broadened in scope to uncover all information related to the company's potential liability. This is an opportunity to address the problem at an early stage and preserve all of the company's options. The company should investigate all plausible leads and review all potentially related documents to ensure there are no other problems.

Several additional underlying factors will affect the scope of the internal investigation, including the following: 1) the number of persons or business units involved in the misconduct; 2) the extent to which mid-level and senior management was involved in, or willfully blind to, the misconduct; 3) the length of time over which the misconduct occured; 4) whether the misconduct affected any government-related services or enforcement efforts; 5) whether the misconduct was prohibited under the company's corporate compliance program; 6) whether a civil lawsuit will likely follow; 7) whether the issue is limited to a human resources problem; and 8) whether there is likely to be adverse publicity.

Ultimately, business judgment and common sense should factor into making the proper determination of the scope of the internal investigation. An internal investigation that lacks these principles can quickly (and easily) go awry—costing a company inordinate amounts of money and possibly increasing its civil and criminal exposure.

Identifying who will conduct the investigation

Who will conduct the investigation is a basic question to be addressed at the start. The company will have to decide whether in-house or outside counsel will run the internal investigation. The considerations for making this determination are discussed in more detail in Chapter Four. In most cases, however, in-house counsel should at least participate in the investigation.

Although counsel will no doubt lead the investigation, usually others will also participate. The investigation team often includes company employees who are "deputized" to assist in the investigation. Identification of appropriate deputies is of utmost importance. First, there can be no possibility that the deputy has any involvement in the subject matter of the investigation. The potential for tainting the entire investigation argues for caution in this area. Similarly, care must be taken when involving people who have direct supervisory or management responsibility over the employees who may be involved in the potential wrongdoing. The internal investigation will ultimately have to address whether there was a lack of appropriate supervision that led to or contributed to the problem. Therefore, a supervisor who is part of the investigation may ultimately be in a position of conflict. It is best to avoid the problem altogether.

The personal character of the potential deputy is also of import. Two important concerns are that the investigation must remain confidential and it must uncover all there is to uncover. The deputy therefore must be trustworthy, discreet and thorough. It also helps for the person to have a good knowledge of the area and people involved.

In addition to a principal deputy, the investigation team may also have to consult with various individuals regarding documents, and information technology personnel regarding electronic documents, especially e-mails. In consulting with such individuals, the confidentiality of the investigation must be emphasized.

Another question is whether to involve a representative of the human resources (HR) department as part of the investigation—specifically as part of the employee interviews. If employment issues are raised, such as discrimination or harassment, it is sometimes helpful to involve the HR department early. It also can put employees at ease to see a familiar face during an interview. Management-labor relations have to be considered in making this determination. It may be appropriate to involve HR in some situations, but not in others. For example, where the issue that has arisen may involve an employment action against the employee, an HR representative may wish to attend. If the issue is solely a health care issue, such a representative need not attend.

Retaining outside consultants

Some internal investigations may require retaining the services of an outside consultant, such as a private investigation firm or forensic accounting firm, to play a role in the investigation. Experienced outside consultants can perform many different and valuable tasks during the internal investigation and their use should be considered from the start. In-house counsel should actively participate in selecting the outside consultant and making important decisions regarding the consultant's analysis of investigatory information.[3]

A health care company should conduct its own due diligence before agreeing to retain a consultant and should not automatically defer to outside counsel's selection. A company should consider the consultant's re-putation for responsiveness, reputation for integrity and independence, experience in handling the type of internal investigation needed by the company, and familiarity with the company's line of business. A company should ask the consultant to provide a list and description of similar investigation projects and the resumes of the investigators who will be participating in the investigation.

Example of types of investigators/consultants

Some investigations may call for a skill set that differs from traditional accounting. Effective forensic accountants are familiar with financial crimes and how to glean evidence of unlawful activity from financial records. They understand that it is not appropriate to assume that a company's figures, numbers and paperwork are honest and correct—they have a high degree of scepticism and treat all documentation as suspect until they prove otherwise. They do not focus on a company's compliance with generally accepted accounting principles, but focus on the details to identify inconsistencies and to resolve anomalies. Medicare cost reporting accountants are critical in both identifying cost reporting issues and in assesing the value of damages. If the issue relates to Medicare coding, it is best to have consultants trained in those issues.

To protect the confidentiality of the internal investigation, consultants should be hired directly by outside counsel, not the company. An engagement letter, which serves a critical role in protecting the confidentiality of an internal investigation, should explicitly state that the consultant is being retained solely to assist outside counsel in rendering legal advice and in the anticipation of litigation, and will be acting at the direction of outside counsel.

The engagement letter must not only set forth the consultant's fees, and the timetable of the investigation, and address liability and indemnification issues, but also set forth certain standardized procedures to preserve the confidentiality of the investigation. For example, the engagement letter should state that the consulting entity must directly report to outside counsel, not the company, via a well understood reporting and supervising chain of command. It should also state that all investigation-related information is to be treated as privileged and confidential and that the consultant is required to immediately report the receipt of any requests or subpoenas for investigation-related information. See Figure 4.2 on page 58.

The consultant should also be given written directions regarding the creation and handling of work product. It must be directed to preface and label all of its investigation-related documentation with an introductory paragraph that prominently indicates that the work product is protected by the attorney-client privilege and work product protection. It is important that the consultant's work product be framed in terms of its opinions and in such a manner that it can be interpreted as protected opinion work product.

The scope of the outside consultant's work must be clearly articulated so that there is a complete demarcation of the duties performed by outside counsel, versus those performed by the consultant. Several ground rules should be set for the consultant at the outset of the investigation. The consultant should be instructed on the scope of its services. The engagement letter should list specific tasks that the consultant is being retained to perform. It should state that the consultant's work product can be performed only at the explicit direction of outside counsel and that the consultant must act within the law and the parameters of legal ethics. It should be made clear that the consultant's role is to provide factual, not legal, analyses and conclusions. The consultant should discuss its analyses and conclusions with outside counsel prior to finalizing them in writing. The consultant should be asked to provide a written explanation of any of its firm's internal lines of authority that might impact the work product.

A health care company is strongly advised not to hire the accounting firm serving as its regular outside auditor to provide consultant services during an internal investigation for three important reasons. First, accounting firms that serve this dual role are most likely ethically proscribed from ignoring troubling information that they obtain during the internal investigation, thereby compromising the confidentiality of the internal investigation. Second, a separate accounting firm will likely have a greater appearance of independence and objectivity in the eyes of prosecutors. Although the company's outside auditor might have a greater familiarity with the company's financial records, the government may suspect that its working relationship with the company's accounting and financial departments will compromise its objectivity. Third, the investigation may concern financial records that the company's auditors reviewed in a prior audit. If this is the case, questions may arise regarding why the auditor did not catch problematic inconsistencies and anomalies. Such tension will hamper the progress of the investigation.

These same considerations apply to consultants in other fields. The company should not hire consultants who regularly perform substantial work for it to assist in the internal investigation.

Identifying legal issues

At the same time the factual investigation is beginning, counsel should be researching the various substantive legal issues that could be involved. A familiarity with the law will enable counsel to determine all the relevant facts. Chapter Three discusses those substantive laws that are likely to apply to internal investigations in the health care industry. It is important to not only read the black and white law, but also to understand the current enforcement attitudes and policies. For those legal issues that are not clear, in certain cases outside counsel can contact the government anonymously to seek clarifications on the regulations.

Coordinating the team

The internal investigation leader must ensure that everyone on the team is working together and that the relevant information is being gathered and analyzed. Any written work product or attorney-client information must be protected. Chapter Four discusses safeguards that must be put into place to ensure that the attorney-client privilege and attorney work product are protected. The leader must also ensure the confidentiality of the entire investigation and avoid sharing incomplete information with non-investigation team members. The leader must guard against spreading rumors and work to ensure that the investigation is completed quickly and efficiently. By ensuring open communications within the team, the decisions will be made with the most information possible.

---

[1] *Most companies' human resources departments are adept at handling employment law issues such as discrimination or harassment claims. We note that particularly difficult employment law issues may also merit a full internal investigation, particularly if they are linked to patient care issues or the credentials of health care professionals.*

[2] *These steps are discussed in detail in Chapter Four.*

[3] *Once the investigation has begun, in-house counsel should periodically coordinate with outside counsel and the investigation's consultant to discuss the status of the consultant's project, investigation timelines, and cost forecasts. Failure to take an active role can result in unnecessary expenses.*

What to look out for—Applicable law

Not every compliance problem that arises will justify an internal investigation. The primary focus of such formal procedures are violations of those state and federal laws that could result in the imposition of serious fines, penalties, or exclusions.

Many providers have a general sense of what problems are most likely to be involved in a health care action—billing for services not rendered or services not medically necessary, double billing, upcoding, or fraudulent cost reporting—but the range of activities specifically prohibited in the health care context might be surprising, if not alarming. From conspiracy to money laundering to RICO, the charges that may be leveled against a provider that is alleged to have defrauded the Medicare program reads more like *True Crime* than *Modern Healthcare*.

Although few providers will garner federal criminal attention, it is important for them to realize that federal enforcement authorities will not need to stretch statutory authority to find a basis to bring criminal charges in a health care case. More common in health care compliance are those civil cases where the government seeks to recoup funds paid erroneously to providers, or to impose financial penalties for unlawful acts. Civil actions may also result in an exclusion or debarment from the Medicare or Medicaid program. Because an exclusion can constitute a "death penalty" for a corporate provider dependent on Medicare revenues, the threat of exclusion often leads providers to settle rather than litigate cases.

While by no means an exhaustive discussion of the applicable provisions that may be applied, this chapter provides an overview of some of the laws, the violation of which might trigger an internal investigation. In addition, see Chapter Eight, "What the Sarbanes-Oxley Act Means to You," which discusses new regulatory provisions that may be applied to publicly traded companies.

Criminal provisions

The Social Security Act

The Social Security Act (SSA) is the source of the Medicare and Medicaid programs. It sets forth an elaborate regulatory structure that governs nearly every aspect of provider operations—including billing, cost reporting, certification, relationships with beneficiaries, and referrals among providers and suppliers. The SSA has provisions that provide criminal sanctions for a broad range of fraudulent acts related to Medicare and Medicaid participation.

The most familiar of these are referred to collectively as the Medicare and Medicaid Anti-Fraud and Abuse Amendments of 1977.[1] Perhaps the best known among the amendments' provisions are those prohibiting false statements and kickbacks. These provisions prohibit the knowing submission of any false statement or representation of a material fact in any application for any benefit or payment of, entitlement to, or retention of any benefits.[2]

The anti-kickback provisions prohibit kickbacks, rebates, and bribes, as well as the payment of any form of remuneration in return for referrals of patients or business for which payment may be made, in whole or in part, under a federal health care program. Also prohibited are any such payments made by those in a position to recommend purchasing, leasing, or ordering any goods, facility, service, or item for which payment may be made under Medicare or Medicaid.[3]

The lesser known criminal provisions of the SSA prohibit a broad range of activities that are in direct contravention of requirements or duties imposed on Medicare providers by the SSA,[4] including the following:

- False statements made in the certification process, including false statements and representations regarding operations and conditions within the facility

- Imposition of charges to Medicaid beneficiaries in excess of allowed amounts, or as a precondition of admission or continued stay in a facility

- Violations of assignment of benefits by participating physicians or suppliers

General criminal statutes frequently applied to health care prosecutions

For many years, government enforcement authorities prosecuting health care cases relied on the criminal provisions generally applicable to federal programs.[5] Examples include criminal provisions prohibiting false claims, such as the following:

- **Mail fraud.**[6] Obtaining money or property through false or fraudulent representations by placing in a post office or authorized mail depository any matter or thing to be sent or delivered by the United States Postal Service.

- **Wire fraud.**[7] Transmitting through wire, radio, or television communication, any false or fraudulent representations designed to defraud or obtain money or property.

- **Criminal RICO statute.**[8] Obtaining funds directly or indirectly from a pattern of racketeering activity. Because mail fraud and wire fraud are predicate offenses and can establish a pattern of racketeering activity, almost any fraud case can be alleged as a RICO case;

- **Conspiracy to defraud the government.**[9] Entering into any agreement, combination, or conspiracy to defraud the federal government by obtaining, or aiding in obtaining, the payment or allowance of any false, fictitious, or fraudulent claim.

- **Submission of fictitious/fraudulent claim.**[10] Making or presenting a claim to any federal department or agency, and knowing such claim to be false, fictitious, or fraudulent.

- **False statements.**[11] Knowingly and willfully: (a) falsifying or concealing a material fact by trick or device; (b) making any materially false, fictitious, or fraudulent statement or representation; or (c) making or using a false writing or document knowing it contains any materially false, fictitious, or fraudulent statement.

Criminal statutes specifically relating to health care fraud

Although prosecutions went forward under these statutes, there was some concern that they did not adequately address the complexity of the Medicare program and the many forms in which claims are submitted for payment under the program. Although those authorities are still available to federal prosecutors, in 1996 Congress passed the Health Insurance Portability and Accountability Act of 1996 (Pub.L.No. 104-191) (HIPAA), which extended the reach of these federal laws to all "health care benefit programs."[12] HIPAA amended Chapter 1 of Title 18 U.S.C., defining the term "federal health care offense" to include violations of, or criminal conspiracies to violate certain federal provisions, if the violation or conspiracy relates to a health care benefit program.

With HIPAA, Congress also gave law enforcement officers a number of new legal weapons to fight health care fraud, including the following provisions:

- Health care fraud,[13] which prohibits any scheme or artifice, false, or fraudulent pretense to defraud a health care program.

- Theft or embezzlement in connection with healthcare,[14] which provides penalties for embezzling, stealing, converting, or misapplying assets of a health care program.

- False statements relating to healthcare matters,[15] which prohibits in any matter involving a federal health care benefit program, knowingly and willfully falsifying, concealing, or covering up a material fact or making any materially false or fraudulent statement or representation.

- Obstruction of criminal investigations of healthcare offenses,[16] which applies to anyone who corruptly, by threat or force, endeavors to influence, intimidate, or impede any witness or willfully prevents, obstructs, misleads, or delays the communication to a criminal investigator of information relating to a federal health care offense.

Civil statutes

Perhaps the most often cited civil law in Medicare enforcement cases is the False Claims Act (FCA).[17] The FCA prohibits the filing of false claims[18] against the government. The FCA is violated by "knowingly" submitting a false claim to the government.

The FCA states that a violation has occurred if a person does any of the following:

- Knowingly presents, or causes to be presented, to an officer or employee of the United States federal government, a false or fraudulent claim for payment or approval

- Knowingly makes, uses, or causes to be made or used, a false record or statement to get a false or fraudulent claim paid or approved by the government

- Conspires to defraud the government through a false or fraudulent claim allowed or paid

- Knowingly makes, uses, or causes to be made or used, a false record or statement to conceal, avoid, or decrease an obligation to pay or transmit money or property to the government

False claims actions will generally be pursued by a United States Attorney. However, under the *qui tam* provisions,[19] the FCA authorizes private individuals called relators to sue, on behalf of the government, persons who knowingly have presented the government with false or fraudulent claims. Relators can then share in any proceeds ultimately recovered as a result of the suit.

Civil provisions

Social Security Act: The civil monetary penalties law

As noted above, the SSA also authorizes the Secretary of Health and Human Services (HHS) to seek civil monetary penalties (CMPs) and assessments, in lieu of, or in addition to, criminal proceedings under the civil monetary penalties law (CMPL).[20] The Secretary of HHS has delegated authority for imposing these civil sanctions to the Office of Inspector General (OIG).

The Secretary is authorized to impose civil money penalties and assessments for a broad range of activities directly related to participation in the Medicare program (42 C.F.R. § 1003.102). The OIG may seek CMPs for actions that are otherwise prohibited under the criminal provisions of the SSA. For example, CMPs may be imposed on a provider who:

- Presents, or causes to be presented, claims to a federal health care program that the person knows or should know are for an item or service that was not provided as claimed, or is false or fraudulent[21]

- Violates the anti-kickback statute[22]

In addition, CMPs may be imposed for violations of specific obligations under the SSA. For example, the OIG may seek CMPs against the following:

- Any hospital emergency department that violates its obligation to provide appropriate medical screening, stabilizing treatment, or an appropriate transfer to any individual who has an emergency medical condition[23]

- A provider that presents a claim that the person knows, or should know, is for a service for which payment may not be made under the physician self-referral or "Stark" law[24]

- A provider that violates the mandatory assignment requirement for certain diagnostic clinical lab tests[25]

- Any supplier that refuses to supply rented DME supplies without charge, after rental payments may no longer be made[26]

The Secretary is authorized to seek different amounts of CMPs and assessments based on the kind of violation at issue.[27]

Exclusions

In most cases for which the Secretary may seek CMPs, he or she may, and in some cases must, exclude offending providers or individuals from participation in all federal health care programs.[28]

Mandatory exclusion

The Secretary must exclude from federal health care program participation any person or entity convicted of: (1) a program-related crime; (2) an offense related to patient neglect or abuse; (3) an offense, related to health care fraud; or (4) a felony related to the unlawful manufacture, distribution, prescription, or dispensing of a controlled substance.[29]

Permissive exclusion

There are two types of permissive exclusions: derivative and non-derivative.[30] Derivative exclusions are those based on prior convictions, sanctions, or penalties. Permissive exclusion may be based on convictions that would not qualify for mandatory exclusion. Derivative exclusions may also be based on the loss of professional licensure, including suspension, revocation, or other loss of licensure, including surrender. Derivative exclusion may also be based on suspension or exclusion from other federal or state health care programs.[31]

Non-derivative exclusions require a *prima facie* showing by the OIG of improper qualifying behavior. The exclusion will be imposed only after the provider is given an opportunity to have a hearing before an Administrative Law Judge (ALJ). Non-derivative exclusions may be based on a wide range of activities.

One category of acts on upon which exclusion may be based is the improper rendering or pricing of services. Specifically, submitting excessive claims and rendering unnecessary services, charging substantially in excess of the provider's usual or normal charges, and the failure to furnish medically necessary services may all justify exclusion.

Non-derivative exclusions may also be based on fraud and kickbacks, or any other violation of the SSA's criminal prohibitions for which CMPs could be imposed.[32] The OIG may also seek to exclude providers that are perceived to be tainted by association with other excluded parties.[33] Specifically, the OIG may exclude entities owned or controlled by a sanctioned individual, and may exclude individuals with ownership in sanctioned entities. Other bases for permissive exclusion include the following:

- Failure to grant immediate access for surveys and audits[34]
- Failure to provide access to subcontractor records[35]
- Defaults on federally-funded education loans[36]

Who prosecutes what?

The investigation and prosecution of fraud and corruption in federal programs is a major priority of the Department of Justice (DOJ), both in the Criminal Division and the Civil Division. United States Attorneys serve as the nation's principal litigators. As such, the United States Attorney's Offices are the focal point for the coordination of criminal and civil health care fraud sanctions.

The client agency of the U.S. Attorney in health care cases is the HHS. U.S. Attorneys will pursue actions on behalf of the HHS, but the agency is responsible for protecting the integrity of its programs, as well as the health and welfare of the beneficiaries of those programs.

The Secretary has delegated much of the responsibility to investigate health care fraud and abuse to the OIG. The OIG's duties are carried out through a nationwide network of audits, investigations, inspections, and other inquiries. The OIG is also charged with administration of the civil and administrative sanctions of the CMPL.

The Medicare and Medicaid Fraud and Abuse Amendments of 1977 authorized the establishment of, and federal funding for, the State Medicaid Fraud Control Units (MFCUs). Currently, 47 states and the District of Columbia participate in the Medicaid Fraud Control Grant Program through their established MFCU. The mission of the Medicaid fraud unit is to investigate and prosecute Medicaid provider fraud and incidences of patient abuse and neglect.

[1] *42 U.S.C. § 1320a-7b, et seq.*

[2] *42 U.S.C. § 1320a-7b(a). This section also applies to anyone who causes false statements to be submitted. Thus, one who supplies false information to be submitted, even if he or she did not submit a claim can be convicted of violating this statute.*

[3] *42 U.S.C. § 1320a-7b(b) (1) and (2).*

[4] *42 U.S.C. § 1320a-7b(c)-(f).*

[5] *See, e.g., 18 U.S.C. § 286, Conspiracy to Defraud the Government With Respect to Claim; 18 U.S.C. § 287, Fictitious or Fraudulent Claims; 18 U.S.C. § 371, Conspiracy to Commit Offense or Defraud; 18 U.S.C. § 494, Contractors, Bonds, Bids, and Public Records; 18 U.S.C. § 495, Contracts, Deeds, and Powers of Attorney; 18 U.S.C. § 1001, False Statements or Entries Generally; 18 U.S.C. § 1002, Possession of False Papers to Defraud United States; 18 U.S.C. § 1341, Mail Fraud; 18 U.S.C. § 1956(c)(7), Laundering of Monetary Instruments; 18 U.S.C. § 1961, Racketeering Influenced and Corrupt Organizations.*

[6] *18 U.S.C. § 1341.*

[7] *18 U.S.C. § 1343.*

[8] *18 U.S.C. §§ 1961-63.*

[9] *18 U.S.C. § 286.*

[10] *18 U.S.C. § 287.*

[11] *18 U.S.C. § 1001.*

[12] *Health care benefit programs are defined to include every public or private plan or contract, affecting commerce, under which any medical benefit, item, or service is provided to any individual. HIPAA also amended Chapter 1 of Title 18 U.S.C. by adding Sec. 24 and defining the term "federal health care offense" to include violations of, or criminal conspiracies to violate, (1) Secs. 669, 1035, 1347, or 1518; and (2) Secs. 287, 371, 664, 666, 1001, 1027, 1341, 1343, or 1954, if the violation or conspiracy relates to a health care benefit program.*

[13] *18 U.S.C. § 1347.*

[14] *18 U.S.C. § 669.*

[15] *18 U.S.C. § 1035.*

[16] *18 U.S.C. § 1518.*

[17] *31 U.S.C. § 3729.*

[18] *This provision is often cited in Medicare cases because "claims" are the primary form of interaction between providers, Medicare, and other federal health care programs. The FCA defines a claim to include "any request or demand . . . for money or property . . . if the United States government provides any portion of the money or property which is requested or demanded." Thus, each Form 1500 or UB-92 claim form, and each cost report, either as a whole or by line-item or itemized service, can be counted as a claim for FCA purposes.*

[19] *31 U.S.C. § 3730.*

[20] *42 U.S.C. § 1320a-7a.*

[21] *42 U.S.C. §§ 1320a- 7a(a)(1)(A) and (B).*

[22] *42 U.S.C. § 1320a-7b(b).*

[23] *42 U.S.C. § 1395dd(d)(1)(A).*

[24] *42 U.S.C. § 1395nn(g)(3).*

[25] *42 U.S.C. §1395l(h).*

[26] *42 U.S.C. §1396 l(i).*

[27] *See 42 C.F.R. § 1003.103.*

[28] *42 U.S.C. § 1320a-7(a), 42 C.F.R.1001.101.*

[29] *42 U.S.C. § 1320a-7(a)(4), 42 C.F.R.1001.101.*

[30] *42 U.S.C. § 1320a-7(b).*

[31] *42 U.S.C. § 320a-7(b)(5).*

[32] *42 U.S.C. § 1320a-7(b)(1).*

[33] *42 U.S.C. § 1320a-7(b)(8) and (15).*

[34] *42 U.S.C. § 1320a-7(b)(12).*

[35] *42 U.S.C. § 1320a-7(b)(10).*

[36] *42 U.S.C. § 1320a-7(b)(14).*

Preserving attorney-client privilege and work-product protection

Introduction

Internal investigations have taken on increased importance in the current enforcement atmosphere, and will likely be the primary means by which health care companies detect wrongdoing and protect their public image and financial welfare. However, successful internal investigations require much skill and diplomacy. Health care companies must conduct investigations in a manner that scrupulously maintains the protections afforded by the attorney-client privilege and work-product protection, while minimizing the potential hazards that may arise during an internal investigation.

The importance of privilege in internal investigations

Corporations conducting internal investigations face two overriding needs: the need to promptly obtain accurate information and respond appropriately; and the need to maintain the confidentiality of the investigation and protect acquired information from undesired disclosure.

Privilege issues often present the thorniest problems for companies conducting internal investigations. Employee interviews, the selection and review of investigation-related documents, the preparation of legal and factual memoranda, and the final investigation report all potentially implicate the attorney-client privilege, work-product protection, and self-evaluative privilege. These protections should be guarded jealously, for decisions implicating them can have a dramatic impact upon the ultimate outcome of an internal investigation.

Attorney-client privilege, work-product protection, and self-evaluative privilege

The attorney-client privilege, work-product protection, and self-evaluative privilege provide three different bases to protect the confidentiality of information that is obtained during an internal investigation. When structuring an investigation, counsel must consider the policy arguments and common-law requirements underlying all three protections. Properly asserting the protections at the outset of the investigation will strengthen later arguments of privilege.

Attorney-client privilege

The attorney-client privilege is one of the "oldest of the privileges for confidential communications known to the common law"[2] and provides almost absolute protection for a limited class of communications. The privilege provides that all communications between an attorney and client that are made for the purpose of obtaining or giving legal advice are confidential.[3] The privilege does not, however, protect the underlying pre-existing facts from disclosure. "A fact is one thing and a communication concerning that fact is an entirely different thing."[4]

Preserving attorney-client privilege and work-product protection

The application of the attorney-client privilege is somewhat more complicated in situations where the client is a corporation. Although corporations are entitled to the same protection of confidentiality as non-corporate clients, the application of the privilege often turns on which corporate officials and employees sufficiently personify the corporation as a client.

In 1981, the Supreme Court provided guidance on the application of the attorney-client privilege in the corporate context—specifically as it regards internal corporate investigations. *Upjohn Co. v. United States*, 449 U.S. 383 (1981), stands for the proposition that the attorney-client privilege and the work-product protection apply to internal investigations by corporations.

In *Upjohn*, company counsel and outside counsel initiated an internal investigation to determine whether the company's foreign subsidiary had violated the Foreign Corrupt Practices Act. Investigating attorneys sent questionnaires to employees seeking detailed information regarding possible illegal overseas payments; the responses to those questionnaires were referred to *Upjohn's* general counsel. Investigating attorneys also interviewed employees and prepared memoranda of those interviews. The Internal Revenue Service then sought the production of the questionnaires, memoranda and interview notes. *Upjohn'* refused to turn over this documentation on the grounds that it was privileged. The district court held that the information was protected.

The Sixth Circuit disagreed, holding that the documentation was not privileged because it did not relate to communications between counsel and the company's "control group" or upper-echelon employees who were "responsible for directing *Upjohn's* actions in response to legal advice."[5] The Supreme Court reversed the appellate court's decision, holding that the privilege could apply to communications made by all *Upjohn* employees to outside counsel in the context of an internal investigation.

Significantly, the Court found that:

> Middle-level and lower-level employees can, by actions within the scope of their employment, embroil the corporation in serious legal difficulties, and it is only natural that these employees would have the relevant information needed by corporate counsel if he or she is adequately to advise the client with respect to such actual or potential difficulties.[6]

The Supreme Court also articulated several factors supporting a claim of attorney-client privilege in connection with employee interviews, including the following:

1) the communications were made by employees pursuant to instructions from superiors in order for the corporation to secure legal advice

2) the information needed by counsel in order to formulate legal advice was not available to senior management

3) the communicated information concerned matters within the employees' duties

4) the employees understood that the purpose of the communication was to enable the corporation to obtain legal advice

5) the communications were ordered to be kept confidential and remained confidential[7]

The decision is not without limits, however. Although *Upjohn* provides broad protection to the confidential communication of all company employees and not just "control-group" or upper-echelon employees, its holding is not universally followed.

In particular, state courts are not bound to follow the *Upjohn* ruling. Different states have different rules regarding the extent to which communication between counsel and company employees is protected by the attorney-client privilege. Some states only provide for the attorney-client privilege when those communications are with the corporation's "control group" or upper-echelon employees.[8] Other states expand the privilege to communications with all company employees who are involved in the subject matter of the investigation.[9] Some states do not even recognize the attorney-client privilege as an absolute prohibition on the disclosure of client confidences.[10]

When conducting internal investigations, health care companies need to be mindful of these differences and the laws of the state where

1) the company is incorporated
2) the company's principal business is conducted
3) the interview is being conducted

Work-product protection

The work-product protection[11] provides qualified immunity to a broad class of communications and documents that are prepared in anticipation of litigation. The purpose of the protection[12] is to provide a lawyer "with a certain degree of privacy, free from unnecessary intrusion by opposing parties and their counsel."[13] In contrast to the attorney-client privilege, which protects only communications, the work-product protection is commonly asserted to preserve the confidentiality of an attorney's mental impressions, conclusions, opinions, or legal theories. The protection also differs from the attorney-client privilege in that it is held by both the client and lawyer.

The work-product protection covers only those materials prepared in "anticipation of litigation" and not for other business purposes, such as public relations or financial auditing. Although collateral use of internal investigation results may muddy the already murky waters of privilege, courts have been willing to consider materials that have been generated during an internal investigation as predicates to litigation, even though litigation may not have ultimately resulted. Therefore, it is imperative that all legal aspects of an internal investigation are fully documented.

Self-evaluative privilege

The "self-evaluative" or "self-critical" privilege, first articulated in *Bredice v. Doctors Hosp, Inc*, 50 F.R.D. 249 (D.D.C. 1970), is designed to encourage parties to engage in candid self-evaluation without fear that such criticism will be used against them. It differs from the attorney-client privilege and work-product protection in that it protects analysis and recommendations that were neither made for the purpose of obtaining or giving legal advice (attorney-client privilege), nor prepared in anticipation of litigation (work-product protection).

Although the self-evaluative privilege may provide alternative legal grounds to protect investigation-related information, it has not been broadly recognized by courts and is subject to numerous exceptions and limitations in those courts where it is recognized. Some courts have held that the privilege may not be asserted against the United States in civil litigation.[14] At least one court has held that the privilege does not apply in *qui tam* actions.[15] In addition, some courts have held that the privilege may be overcome by a showing of exceptional necessity or if other interests (such as public policy interests) outweigh the underlying interest of the privilege.[16] In general, health care companies should not place too much reliance on this doctrine to protect results from internal investigations.

Preserving the confidentiality of internal investigations

The attorney-client privilege, work-product protection, and self-evaluative privilege are generally asserted to protect the confidentiality of communications and materials associated with internal investigations. Confidentiality is not, however, automatically preserved during an internal investigation, even in situations where the internal investigation is being conducted by attorneys. The attorney-client privilege, work-product protection, and self-evaluative privilege can be deliberately or inadvertently waived. These lapses can be avoided if certain formalities are consistently adhered to from the initiation of the investigation.

Waiver of the privilege

Waiver issues frequently arise in situations where fruits of an internal investigation are shared with the government during settlement negotiations. The circuits are currently split as to whether disclosure of investigation-related information results in a limited waiver of the shared information (the minority rule), or a broad waiver of potentially every document related to the subject matter of the disclosed information (the majority rule).

Subject matter waivers

In 1988, the Fourth Circuit caused an uproar within the legal community when it held that a company that had appeared to follow the *Upjohn* procedures had waived the attorney-client privilege and the protection of non-opinion work product in the context of resolving a criminal prosecution of the corporation. See *In re Martin Marietta Corp.*, 856 F.2d 619 (4th Cir. 1988), *cert. denied*, 490 U.S. 1011 (1989). In *Martin Marietta*, the court found that an implied waiver of the attorney-client privilege and non-opinion work-product protection had occurred when the company settled criminal and administrative charges with the Department of Defense (DOD).

The government's case against Martin Marietta involved improperly recorded travel cost rebates that were reported to the DOD. During settlement negotiations, Martin Marietta's counsel disclosed limited confidential information to the government. The company was ultimately indicted, entered a guilty plea, and concurrently settled the administrative proceedings. Shortly thereafter, an employee who was separately charged with conspiracy to defraud and mail fraud issued a pretrial subpoena *duces tecum* to the company pursuant to Federal Rule of Criminal Procedure 17(c). The subpoena sought Martin Marietta's internal audit, interview notes, transcripts, and recordings on which the audit's findings were based, and correspondence and notes concerning the administrative settlement.

Martin Marietta resisted demands to produce the documentation on the grounds that its submission to the government constituted only a limited waiver of the attorney-client privilege and work-product protection. The Fourth Circuit rejected the "limited waiver" concept and ordered the production of all of the underlying source documents, not just the documentation disclosed to the government. The court did, however, afford greater protection under the work-product protection and remanded the case for further determination of the protection's applicability.

Several courts have granted subject matter waivers since the *Martin Marietta* decision.[17] Although the law in this area is far from settled, health care companies should be aware that disclosure of investigation-related information to the government will raise significant waiver issues.

Health care companies should also be aware that inadvertent disclosures of investigation-related information to the government may raise significant concerns about waiver. Two circuits have specifically held that a broad subject matter waiver may apply in inadvertent disclosures to the government. In *In* re Sealed Case, 877 F.2d 976, 980-81 (D.C. Cir. 1989), the District of Columbia Circuit stated that inadvertent disclosure waives attorney-client privilege to "all communications related to the same subject matter." The Third Circuit confirmed this holding in In re Grand Jury, 138 F.3d 978, 978-82 (3d Cir. 1998), but qualified the waiver as occurring only when the party with the privilege did not in a timely manner assert the privilege to the government, in that case, for four months.

The issue of waiver must also be anticipated in situations where a confidentiality agreement is involved. In Westinghouse Elec. Corp. v. Republic of the Philippines, 951 F.2d 1414, 1421-30 (3d Cir. 1991), the Third Circuit ruled unequivocally that Westinghouse's disclosure of documents from an internal investigation to the SEC and the Department of Justice waived any attorney-client privilege or work-product protection in those materials. The waiver occurred despite the government's agreement to maintain the confidentiality of the information and to not retain any copies of the documents. Although the Second Circuit suggested in In re Steinhardt Partners, 9 F.3d 230, 236 (2d Cir. 1993), that the attorney-client privilege and non-opinion work product may be protected by confidentiality agreements, recent cases have followed the Third Circuit's lead in finding waivers regardless of confidentiality agreements.[18] Decisions to produce privileged material to the government must be carefully examined for problems that may occur in future civil litigation.

Employment law issues

A company that conducts an internal investigation in response to allegations of harassment or discrimination must carefully consider the strong possibility of having to waive the attorney-client privilege, work-product protection or self-evaluative privilege. If the internal investigation is used as an affirmative defense, the company must be prepared to waive all of its privileges related to the investigation. Asserting that the company acted reasonably, took appropriate remedial steps, and/or accommodated the claimant pursuant to the results of an internal investigation will result in a full subject-matter waiver of the attorney-client privilege and the work product associated with the investigation.[19] This includes waiver of all notes relating to the investigation and the entire investigative report.[20] If a company chooses to not assert the investigation as a defense, the attorney-client privilege and work-product protection remain intact.

Determining whether to use in-house or outside counsel

After it has been decided that an internal investigation is appropriate, the next question is whether to use in-house or outside counsel to conduct that investigation. The principal reasons for using in-house counsel are their greater familiarity with the company's business practices and personnel, the desire to minimize interference with the normal operations of the business, and a need to minimize cash expenditures for counsel fees.

Most often, however, it is still in a company's best interest to use outside counsel—especially in situations where the allegations of wrongdoing are serious. The principal reasons for using outside counsel, particularly where alleged or suspected misconduct by employees is involved, are as follows:

- The need to complete an investigation within a limited time frame or to a depth that is beyond the resources of in-house counsel

- Avoidance of actual or potential conflicts of interest or other personal inhibitions that in-house counsel might experience

- Outside counsel's greater experience in criminal defense work and previously established rapport with the prosecutors

- The greater appearance of independence and objectivity outside counsel's work have in the eyes of prosecutors and administrators.

In-house counsel are often asked to provide both legal advice (which is privileged) and business advice (which is not). Outside counsel are not impaired by this blurring of responsibilities, and are in a better position to structure the investigation in a manner best calculated to preserve the attorney-client privilege and work-product protection.

The most favored approach, which draws on the strengths of both counsel, assigns senior counsel within the company to work closely with outside counsel, who actually control the investigation. This strategy enables the company to take advantage of in-house counsel's greater familiarity with the workings of the company and outside counsel's experience with the criminal law process.

Practical recommendations for protecting the confidentiality of internal investigations

Certain standard procedures should be followed regardless of whether in-house or outside counsel conducts the investigation in order for the attorney-client privilege, work-product protection, and self-evaluative privilege to remain intact. These procedures should be understood by all involved before the investigation is initiated to avoid waiver of these protections.

Early attorney involvement

The attorney-client privilege and the work-product protection do not apply if information is obtained without or before lawyer involvement. Consequently, company compliance programs should require senior and mid-level management to promptly notify in-house counsel of all potential improprieties so that a reasoned legal decision can be made as to whether an investigation should be initiated.

Senior management should be firmly discouraged from going on non-privileged fact-finding missions—especially in the form of demands for immediate answers addressed to junior management. Such inquiries would not be protected by privilege and may yield results inconsistent with the internal investigation. In addition, these activities may create an appearance of "head-hunting," which drains morale and can create disincentives for candor.

Engagement letters

The next step in preserving an investigation's confidentiality is to formally engage outside counsel to conduct the investigation. The nature and scope of the engagement must be clearly stated in writing to avoid any possible misunderstanding that may arise with employee turnover and the passage of time. It is important to memorialize that legal advice is being sought so that privileges and protections are not successfully challenged on the grounds that the internal investigation did not have a primarily legal purpose.

To memorialize that legal advice is being sought through an internal investigation, the board of directors (or some other senior executive decision-making body) should issue written authorization that reflects that counsel is being sought to assess possible legal exposure rather than a purely factual inquiry. The written authorization should

1) clearly state that the goal of the internal investigation is to obtain legal, and not business, advice

2) distinguish between the legal and purely business objectives of the investigation

3) refer to specific business practices that are thought to have raised potential legal issues

4) state that counsel's communications and all products of the investigation are intended to be protected by the attorney-client privilege and work-product protection

5) stress the need for confidentiality and inform outside counsel that they have access to all company resources and personnel necessary to conduct the inquiry

See sample board resolution, attached hereto as Figure 4.1.

FIGURE 4.1

SAMPLE BOARD RESOLUTION

COMPANY X

ACTION BY UNANIMOUS WRITTEN CONSENT
OF THE
BOARD OF DIRECTORS
Dated: May 31, 2003

THE UNDERSIGNED, being the entire Board of Directors (the "Board") of Company X, a Pennsylvania corporation (the "Company"), in accordance with the authority contained in Section XXXX of the Pennsylvania Business Corporation Law, as amended, and Section XXX of the Company's Bylaws, **DO HEREBY CONSENT** in writing that the following resolutions shall have the same force and effect as if duly adopted at a meeting of the Board, duly called and held in accordance with the law and the Bylaws of the Company.

Initiation of Internal Investigation

RESOLVED, that, as this Board deems it to be in the best interests of this Company and its shareholders, the General Counsel of the Company be, and hereby is authorized on behalf of this Board, to engage the services of Hospital Lawyer, LLP (the "Firm") to conduct a confidential investigation and inquiry into matters related to the Company's **[INSERT DESCRIPTION]** for purposes of discovering and eliciting facts, making certain findings, and providing to the Board a report containing the legal opinion and legal advice of the Firm, so that the Board may properly discharge its duties.

FURTHER RESOLVED, that the Firm be, and hereby is authorized, to obtain assistance as may be reasonably required in this inquiry from outside consultants to conclude in a prompt and diligent manner the above commissioned inquiry and investigation.

FURTHER RESOLVED, that this Board delegates to the General Counsel the power and authority to review this matter in detail with the Firm and, where necessary and appropriate, to provide the Firm any necessary interim authorization or

FIGURE
4.1

SAMPLE BOARD RESOLUTION (CONT.)

advice that may be necessary or desirable for the efficient handling and conclusion of the above mentioned inquiry and investigation.

FURTHER RESOLVED, that the officers and directors of this Company be, and are hereby directed, to cooperate fully with and insure that all employees of this Company cooperate fully with the Firm and any other such persons that the Firm may retain in the foregoing matters.

FURTHER RESOLVED, that the Board of Directors designates the Firm as an agent of the Company for purposes of the indemnification provisions of the Company's by-laws, and instructs its General Counsel to prepare an indemnification agreement between the Company and the Firm, satisfactory to the Firm in order to assure that the Firm has maximum protection against the cost and expense of defending any lawsuit against it which arises out of its conduct of this investigation.

General

FURTHER RESOLVED, that the proper officers of the Company be, and such officers are, hereby authorized, empowered, and directed in the name and on behalf of the Company, to take such other action as they may deem necessary or desirable to carry out the intent and purpose of the foregoing resolution, with the execution and delivery or other action by any such officer constituting evidence of such approval.

FURTHER RESOLVED, that all actions heretofore taken consistent with the purposes and intents of the foregoing resolutions be, and each of them is, in all respects hereby approved, ratified, and confirmed.

FURTHER RESOLVED, that this Action By Unanimous Written Consent may be executed in one or more counterparts and when each Director has executed at least one counterpart, the foregoing resolutions shall be deemed adopted and in full force and effect as of the date hereof. The appropriate officer of the

FIGURE
4.1

SAMPLE BOARD RESOLUTION (CONT.)

Company is hereby directed to file a signed copy of this Consent in the minute book of the Company.

IN WITNESS WHEREOF, all of the members of the Board have executed this Unanimous Written Consent of Directors of the Company as of the date hereof.

[SIGNATURES TO UNANIMOUS WRITTEN CONSENT OF BOARD OF DIRECTORS]

_____   _____
Director A   Director B

_____   _____
Director C   Director D

CONSTITUTING THE ENTIRE BOARD OF DIRECTORS

Filed with the minutes of proceedings of the Board of Directors of Company X by the undersigned as Secretary of the Company on the day and year set forth above. I do hereby certify that the directors executing the foregoing document constitute all the directors of Company X, entitled to express consent or dissent in writing to the foregoing corporate actions at the time such document was filed with me.

_____
Secretary of Company X

Outside counsel should, in turn, confirm the request to conduct the privileged investigation in writing. This confirmation should take the form of a detailed letter or memorandum that addresses the above-mentioned issues. See sample engagement letter, attached hereto as Figure 4.2.

Written requests for company cooperation

Uncounseled statements to government investigators or reporters can both increase a company's exposure to civil or criminal liability and inadvertently obviate the attorney-client privilege. It is often necessary to inform certain company employees that the company has initiated an internal investigation and direct them on how to conduct themselves accordingly.

Keeping employees aware of the sensitive nature of the situation helps squelch rumors and preserves employee morale. Such an announcement may also prevent employees from being surprised if ever contacted by government agents outside of the workplace.

Employees can be notified of an ongoing investigation through a simple memorandum. A senior company executive should distribute a memorandum to relevant employees and executives of the company, informing them that an investigation has been initiated and requesting their cooperation. This memorandum should emphasize the need to maintain the confidentiality of the investigation. It should state that all personnel should report investigation-related information to designated counsel—not their usual chain of command. The memorandum should also tell company personnel that they are not required to speak with government investigators without counsel being present, and that they must speak to designated counsel prior to responding to governmental and/or media inquiries. See sample memorandum to employees, attached hereto as Figure 4.3.

FIGURE
4.2

SAMPLE ENGAGEMENT LETTER

Attorney A
111-111-1111
attorneya@hospitallawyer.com

**PRIVILEGED AND CONFIDENTIAL
ATTORNEY–CLIENT COMMUNICATION**

June 1, 2003

XXXXXXXX
Chief Executive Officer
Company X
1040 Being Investigated Street
Philadelphia, PA XXXXX

Re: Confidential Internal Investigations

Dear XXXX:

This will confirm that Company X ("the Company") has engaged Hospital Lawyer, LLP (also "the Firm") to conduct a confidential internal investigation related to the Company's **[INSERT DESCRIPTION]**.

The purpose of this investigation is to gather information for this Firm to use in providing Company X with legal advice, including advice in anticipation of a potential criminal or civil investigation. All communications and products of this confidential investigation are intended to be protected by the attorney-client privilege and work-product protection.

We understand that the Firm has the authority to interview company representatives and obtain any other information necessary to accomplish this objective. In addition, this Firm may enlist company personnel to assist us during the course of the investigation. However, in order to preserve applicable privileges, it is imperative that Company X personnel not take any investigative steps, including conducting interviews or gathering documentary or other information, except in consultation with us.

As discussed above, the conduct and results of our investigation will be confidential. We will report the progress and results of the investigation to **[LAWYER NAME]** and coordinate our activities with you.

Very truly yours,

Attorney A

FIGURE 4.3

SAMPLE MEMORANDUM TO EMPLOYEES

[Company X letterhead]

To: Company X Employees
From: Senior Company Executive
Subject: Government Investigation

[Insert description of agency conducting investigation] is currently conducting an investigation related to **[insert description]**. The company intends to cooperate with the investigation to the fullest extent possible, and hopes that the matter will be resolved soon. We also ask that you maintain the confidentiality of this investigation and provide your full cooperation.

There is a possibility that a government investigator or media reporter may seek to interview Company X employees as part of this investigation. We want you to have a clear understanding of your rights and obligations if you are contacted.

1. You have the right to be interviewed. You may also decline to be interviewed. You cannot be forced by the government to give any statement except under oath and pursuant to a valid subpoena.

2. You have the right to consult with an attorney in order to decide whether to be interviewed.

3. If you are contacted by a government investigator and you decide to speak to him or her, you have the right to speak with an attorney before and during each and every conversation that you have with the government investigator. You are also entitled to have an attorney with you during any conversations that you may have with government investigators.

4. If you are contacted by a government investigator or media reporter, we ask that you immediately notify me at _____. In addition, Company X has hired the law firm of Hospital Lawyer, LLP to advise and assist the company with this investigation. Attorney A of Hospital Lawyer, LLP is

FIGURE
4.3 SAMPLE MEMORANDUM TO EMPLOYEES (CONT.)

available to answer any questions that you might have. You may contact Attorney A at XXX-XXX-XXXX or at home at XXX-XXX-XXXX.

5. If you decide to be interviewed by a government investigator, you must provide full and truthful information in response to any questions you choose to answer. You should be aware that, while you are not required to provide information, you can be prosecuted if you provide information that is untrue or misleading.

6. It is your decision whether you want to speak to government investigators. We do, however, urge you to consult with an attorney before you have any discussions with any government investigators.

Thank you for your cooperation.

XXXXXXXXXXXXXX
Senior Company Executive

Directives to company investigators

A typical investigation usually requires a team. Many internal investigations involve non-attorney employees and outside consultants[21] in important coordinating or supervisory roles (see Chapter one). These individuals may be asked to assist in discrete aspects of the investigation or may be more integrally involved in the investigation. To preserve the attorney-client privilege and work-product protection, however, certain standardized procedures must be followed, irrespective of the extent of their involvement.

If outside consultants are used, these individuals should be hired directly by outside counsel and report directly to outside counsel to preserve the attorney-client privilege and work-product protection. The engagement letter between the consultants and outside counsel should explicitly state that the consultants are being retained to assist outside counsel in rendering legal advice. See sample retention letter, attached hereto as Figure 4.4.

FIGURE 4.4 **Sample retention letter**

Attorney A

|||-|||-||||

attorneya@hospitallawyer.com

**PRIVILEGED AND CONFIDENTIAL
ATTORNEY–CLIENT COMMUNICATION**

June 1, 2003

BY HAND DELIVERY

Company Investigator A
Company Investigator Incorp.
1040 Investigation Street
Philadelphia, PA XXXXX

Re: Confidential Internal Investigation

Dear XXXXX:

This letter will confirm the arrangement by which you have agreed to undertake work for Hospital Lawyer, LLP (also "the Firm") in regard to the above-referenced matter.

The Firm has been retained to render legal services to Company X (the "Company") in connection with **[INSERT DESCRIPTION]**. The purpose of this investigation is to gather information for this Firm to use in providing legal advice to the Company, including advice in anticipation of a potential criminal investigation.

In connection with this matter, we have express authority to retain consultants as appropriate to work with and report directly to us. This work contemplates services of a character and quality that are a necessary adjunct to our legal services, and that will assist us in performing such services for the Company, including providing advice in anticipation of litigation.

With respect to any work performed by Company Investigator A on behalf of the Firm in connection with this representation, we have agreed as follows:

1. That, henceforth, unless otherwise notified in writing, you shall work with, receive directions from, and report directly to the Firm.

FIGURE
4.4

Sample retention letter (cont.)

2. All communications between you, anyone associated with your firm, or anyone working under your supervision (collectively referred to as "you"), and any attorney, agent, or employee of the Company shall be regarded as confidential and made solely for the purpose of assisting counsel in providing legal advice to the Company.

3. All workpapers, records, or other documents, regardless of their nature and the course from which they emanate, shall be held by you solely for our convenience and subject to our unqualified right to instruct you with respect to possession and control. Any such papers prepared by you or under your direction belong to this Firm.

4. All communications, workpapers, and related documents are subject to the Company's attorney-client privilege and the work-product protection. They should be prefaced with an introductory paragraph that states that they have been produced at the direction of the Firm, and designed to assist counsel in rendering legal advice to the Company and should be marked with the following:

**PRIVILEGED AND CONFIDENTIAL:
ATTORNEY-CLIENT PRIVILEGE/ATTORNEY WORK PRODUCT**

5. Without our advance written permission, you will not:

   (a) disclose the nature or content of any oral or written communication between or among you, this Firm, and/or the Company;

   (b) disclose any information gained from the inspection of any record or document submitted to you, including information obtained from business records or documents;

   (c) disclose any information coming into your possession during the performance of services on our behalf;

   (d) make reproductions of any investigator notes or reports; or

   (e) permit the inspection of any papers or documents by any third party.

FIGURE
4.4

SAMPLE RETENTION LETTER (CONT.)

6. As part of this agreement, you will immediately notify the Firm of the occurrence of any one of the following events:

   (a) the exhibition or surrender of any documents or records created by or submitted to you or someone under your direction, in a manner not expressly authorized by the Firm;

   (b) a request by anyone to examine, inspect, or copy any such documents or records; or

   (c) any attempt to serve, or the actual service of, any court order, subpoena, or summons upon you which requires the production of any such documents or records.

Additionally, you will immediately return all documents, records, and work papers to us upon our request.

7. You will charge for your services based on an hourly rate of $XXX. In addition to this hourly rate, you will bill at cost all reasonable business expenses incurred on our behalf, including, but not limited to, long-distance telephone charges, photocopying, faxing, parking, and travel costs, and other similar expenditures. You are to remit all bills to the Company directly for payment. A concurrent copy of such bills should also be forwarded to the Firm.

If you are in agreement with these terms, please sign the enclosed copy of this letter and return it to me.

We look forward to working with you on this matter.

Very truly yours,

Attorney A

AGREED TO AND ACCEPTED: _____

COMPANY A INVESTIGATOR

Preserving attorney-client privilege and work-product protection

Although involving company employees in the internal investigation has several practical advantages, these advantages must be weighed against concerns about inadvertent waiver. Efforts should be made to limit the number of company employees involved in the investigation and to limit disclosure of investigation-related information only to those necessary for providing legal advice to the company. Employees who are involved in the investigation should also be supervised by outside counsel to avoid the inadvertent waiver of privilege. The bulk of the investigatory work should also be handled by attorneys who must make legal determinations based on subtle factual distinctions.

Inadvertent waiver can be minimized if persons working on the investigation receive written instruction from counsel that

1) describes the general contours of the investigation (e.g., the caption of the case and what division or products are involved), and the scope of their participation

2) instructs them that they have been asked to assist the lawyers conducting the investigation, and that all work must be performed at the direction of those attorneys

3) directs them to report directly to a designated attorney and not their usual chain of command

4) instructs them to treat all investigation-related information as privileged and confidential

5) forbids them from discussing any investigation-related information with others, including other personnel, without obtaining advance written permission, even after their termination from the company/outside consulting firm

6) directs them to preface all investigation-related documents with an introductory paragraph that states that they have produced, at the direction of counsel, and designed to assist counsel in rendering legal advice to the company

7) instructs them that they should not make copies of their notes or reports, but should deliver all originals and work papers to a designated attorney

8) prohibits them from allowing the inspection of any investigation-related documents by any third party without advance written permission

9) requires them to immediately inform a designated attorney of any attempts by third parties to obtain investigation-related information, or if there has been an inadvertent release of investigation-related materials to third parties

Once the information-gathering phase of the internal investigation has begun, persons who are involved in the investigation should also be provided with a list of individuals permitted to gain access to investigative materials and information.

Collecting investigation documents

One of the principal components of an internal investigation is identifying and understanding the relevant documents. This also must be done in a manner that minimizes the possibility of waiver of the attorney-client privilege and work-product protection.

At the outset, an effort should be made to identify the general categories of relevant documents, and a request issued to various departments or divisions that may have these documents. This can be accomplished by a memorandum from a senior corporate official that requests this documentation and explains that the request was made by counsel, and for counsel's utilization.

Counsel should also keep a privilege log. One attorney should be responsible for reviewing all documentation that is included on the log, because an inconsistent position may result in an inadvertent waiver. Special steps may also be necessary to prevent the alteration or destruction of pertinent documents.

Conducting employee interviews[22]

Interviews of company employees need to be handled sensitively to minimize the possibility of waiver of the attorney-client privilege and work-product protection. This can be accomplished through the implementation of a few precautionary measures.

First, interviewed employees must be told at the beginning of the interview that the interviewing attorney represents the company and not the employee, and that the purpose of the interview is to allow the attorney to formulate legal advice to the company. Telling the employee this will help avoid the claim that the interviewed employee holds the privilege, and therefore has the power to waive it or preclude the company from waiving it. Second, the interviewing attorney must also be clear that the interview is privileged and must be kept confidential in order to minimize the possibility of inadvertent waiver. Third, the interviewing attorney should not use any privileged documents during the interview to refresh the employee's recollection, for doing so could constitute waiver. The interviewing attorney should not ask the witness to review or adopt his or her notes or interview memorandum.

Controlling the flow of information

In determining whether there has been a waiver of the attorney-client privilege or work-product protection, courts have considered the degree of care that a company used to ensure the confidentiality of internal investigation information. A company can demonstrate the intended confidentiality of this information by:

1) requiring non-lawyers to report investigation-related information directly to counsel, and not through the regular chain of command

2) seeking information from the highest possible sources within the company, and contacting lower-level employees as a last recourse

3) requiring that all investigation-related materials are clearly marked with a readily identifiable legend at the top of each page that reads **"PRIVILEGED AND CONFIDENTIAL ATTORNEY-CLIENT/WORK PRODUCT. DO NOT DUPLICATE"**

4) limiting the dissemination of all investigation-related documents, and requiring that investigation-related documents be numbered

5) requiring all recipients of investigation-related documents to return these documents to counsel at the conclusion of the investigation

6) maintaining investigation files in a separate location from general corporate files, and limiting access to these files

7) storing all electronic investigation-related data on a separate database from general corporate electronic data, and limiting access to this data

Dealing with third-party inquiries

The responsibility for responding to press and government inquiries should be clearly established to avoid inadvertent waiver. If the corporation has an in-house public relations department, a senior representative of that department should be designated to respond to press inquiries after consulting with in-house counsel. Responses to government inquiries that relate in any fashion to the subject matter of the investigation must also be coordinated through in-house counsel to ensure that inconsistent or inaccurate statements are not made.

Drafting and distributing the investigation report

After the internal investigation has concluded, it may be decided that a written report should be given to the company's board of directors (or some other senior executive decision-making body). If a written report is necessary, this report should contain as realistic an analysis as possible, and only information that is absolutely necessary is to be committed to writing. It should also be marked as confidential. The report should also be in a format that maximizes the protections of the attorney-client privilege and work-product protection. This can be accomplished by including the following components:

1) A description of the investigative process, including why and by whom, how the investigation was conducted, and what issues were explored

2) A detailed summary of the facts

3) An analysis of applicable legal principles

4) An identification of perceived weaknesses in the company's practices and procedures

5) A review of the potential administrative and criminal sanctions

6) An outline of the arguments against those sanctions and criminal prosecution

7) Recommendations of corrective action to cure the deficiencies and enhance the company's administrative and criminal defenses

Although an investigation report that is prepared for external disclosure may differ somewhat from a report that is prepared for internal purposes, it must be consistent on all material points with any internal report. Such a report should include the following components:

1) An introduction addressing how and why the investigation was begun, by whom it was conducted, over what time period, and what issue(s) it addressed

2) A description of the investigative process, set forth in a fashion designed to show its thoroughness (for example, enumerating the number of documents reviewed and interviews conducted)

3) A summary of the pertinent factual findings

4) A description of any corrective actions taken, with emphasis on how they will help prevent the problem from recurring

5) A brief description of any disciplinary actions taken (probably without names)

6) Any financial action that the company has taken or intends to take (for example, refunds or restitution to customers)

Care should be taken in deciding how to disseminate the report, irrespective of its intended audience; all copies should also be securely maintained. Internal reports, if possible, should also only be distributed to the board of directors (or some other senior executive decision-making body).

The Department of Justice's revised principles of the prosecution of business organizations

On January 20, 2003, United States Deputy Attorney General Larry D. Thompson released a memorandum, titled "Principles of Federal Prosecution of Business Organizations,"[23] that confirms an ongoing cultural and legal shift in the federal government's attitude toward prosecuting corporations. It also sets a high bar with respect to waiver of the attorney-client privilege and the work-product protection for companies seeking to avoid prosecution by cooperating with the government. This shift will continue to have a dramatic effect on the way in which internal investigations are conducted, since the fruits of those investigations stand a substantial chance of being surrendered to the government.

The revised principles state that a company's "timely and voluntary disclosure of wrongdoing and its willingness to cooperate with the government's investigation may be relevant factors" when the Justice Department is determining whether to charge it with a crime.[24] When gauging the extent of a company's cooperation, a prosecutor may consider the corporation's willingness to disclose the complete results of its internal investigation, and to waive the attorney-client privilege and work-product protection.[25]

One positive factor the prosecutor may weigh in assessing the adequacy of a corporation's cooperation is the completeness of its disclosure. Conversely, partial or misleading disclosures can complicate relationships. This includes, if necessary, a waiver of the attorney-client and work-product protections, both with respect to its internal investigation and with respect to communications between specific officers, directors, and employees and counsel. Such waivers permit the government to obtain statements of possible witnesses, subjects, and targets, without having to negotiate individual cooperation or immunity agreements. In addition, they are often critical in enabling the government to evaluate the completeness of a corporation's voluntary disclosure and cooperation.[26]

Although the revised principles state that the Justice Department does not consider the waiver of the attorney-client privilege and/or work-product protection to be an absolute requirement, the department has been increasingly pressuring companies to waive the attorney-client privilege and work-product protection for communications relating to internal investigations, and contemporaneous legal advice associated with those investigations as a condition of cooperation.[27] A company's refusal to waive the privilege or protection, at a minimum, is viewed with deep suspicion by federal investigators and, at worst, as a "clandestine effort to hide the truth." In addition, the sentencing guidelines reward voluntary disclosure and cooperation with a reduction in a corporation's offense level.[28] The reality and impact of an impending criminal charge may leave a company with little choice but to accede to the government's demand that the privilege and protection be waived.[29]

Publicly held corporations in particular face a Hobson's choice when it comes to waiver. Once the privilege or protection is waived, there is virtually no way to reassert it. This raises serious concerns in light of potential civil liability, including shareholder derivative and class-action suits even if there is ultimately no criminal liability.

A health care company can, however, limit the damage that might be caused by a possible limited waiver if it carefully thinks through and plans each internal investigation with this issue in mind. If the company uncovers troubling conduct that might result in voluntary disclosure or becomes the subject of the federal government's scrutiny, it can carefully organize and conduct its ensuing internal investigation and document the legal advice that is provided, related to that investigation.

Part of this strategy may involve the preparation of two sets of work product. One set would contain only facts from the investigation (e.g., witness interview memoranda). The other would contain legal advice and impressions (e.g., impressions of witnesses' credibility, strategies for utilizing the information obtained during the investigation, or liability analyses). A company may also want to negotiate the issuance of a subpoena to safeguard privileges and protections. Some companies may choose to forego written reports of investigation findings (including the final report) to limit potential discovery by third-party litigants.

In this enforcement atmosphere, health care companies are well advised to take into account the very real possibility that their investigation findings and conclusions may be disclosed to the government during settlement negotiations. Investigation policies and procedures must be crafted accordingly. The ultimate decision will come down to a judgment call based on the unique facts of each case. That decision should be made in consultation with counsel who are well versed in the applicable privilege laws and experienced in conducting internal investigations.

[1] See Press Release, Dept. of Health and Human Serv. – Office of Inspector Gen., "OIG Saves Taxpayers Record $21 Billion" (Dec. 11, 2002).

[2] Upjohn Co. v. United States, 449 U.S. 383, 398 (1981).

[3] See United States v. United Shoe Mach. Corp., 89 F. Supp. 357 (D. Mass. 1950).

[4] Upjohn, 449 U.S. at 395-96 (1981).

[5] United States v. Upjohn Co., 600 F.2d 1223, 1225 (6th Cir. 1979).

[6] Upjohn, 449 U.S. at 391.

[7] Id. at 394-95.

[8] See, e.g., Consolidation Coal Co. v. Bucyrus-Erie Co., 432 N.E.2d 250 (Ill. 1982).

[9] See, e.g., Southern Bell Tel. & Tel. Co. v. Deason, 632 So. 2d 1377 (Fla. 1994).

[10] See, e.g., Leonen v. Johns-Manville, 135 F.R.D. 94, 98 (D.N.J. 1990) ("[w]hile the federal attorney-client privilege is absolute, the New Jersey state privilege is qualified").

[11] Courts have distinguished between "opinion" work product and "factual" work product. Opinion work product consists of the attorney's mental impressions, conclusions, opinions, and legal theories. Such information is covered by the protection. Factual work product consists of the underlying facts of the investigation – this information is not covered by the protection.

[12] The work-product protection is also codified at Rule 26(b)(3) of the Federal Rules of Civil Procedure, which provides, in relevant part:

> [A] party may obtain discovery of documents and tangible things . . . prepared in anticipation of litigation . . . only upon a showing that the party seeking discovery has a substantial need of the materials . . . and that he is unable to obtain the substantial equivalent of the materials by other means . . . [T]he court shall protect against the disclosure of the mental impressions, conclusions, opinions, or legal theories of an attorney or other representative of a party concerning the litigation.

[13] Hickman v. Taylor, 329 U.S. 495, 510 (1947).

[14] See, e.g., Federal Trade Comm'n v. TRW Inc., 628 F.2d 207, 210 (D.C. Cir. 1980) (citations omitted).

[15] See, e.g., United States ex rel Falsetti v. Southern Bell Tel. & Tel. Co., 915 F. Supp. 308, 313 (N.D. Fla. 1996).

[16] See, e.g., Mewborn v. Heckler, 101 F.R.D. 691, 692-93 (D.D.C. 1984) (citations omitted).

[17] See In re Sealed Case, 877 F.2d 976, 980-81 (D.C. Cir. 1989) (disclosure to the government, even inadvertent disclosure, waives attorney-client privilege "to all other communications relating to the same subject matter"); Neal v. Honeywell, Inc., 1995 WL 591461, *5-7 (N.D. Ill. Oct. 4, 1995) (voluntary disclosure to the government waives attorney-client privilege and non-opinion work-product protection to all materials relating to the same subject matter); In re Leslie Fay Cos. Sec. Litig., 161 F.R.D. 274, 282-84 (S.D.N.Y. 1995) (voluntary disclosure of audit committee's report to SEC waives attorney-client privilege as to all materials relating to the same subject mat-

ter); United States ex rel. Mayman v. Martin Marietta Corp., 886 F. Supp. 1243, 1251-52 (D. Md. 1995) (attorney-client privilege waived as to all communications on the subject matter); United States v. Massachusetts Inst. of Tech., 129 F.3d 681 (1st Cir. 1997) (voluntary disclosure of information to government waives attorney-client privilege as to all materials relating to the subject matter).

[18] See e.g., Cooper Hosp./Univ. Med. Center v. Sullivan, 183 F.R.D. 119, 131-37 (D.N.J. 1998) (disclosing information to the government resulted in a full subject-matter waiver of work product notwithstanding confidentiality agreement).

[19] See Sealy v. Gruntal & Co., 1998 WL 698257, *5 (S.D.N.Y. 1998); Johnson v. Rauland-Borg Corp., 961 F. Supp. 208, 211 (N.D. Ill. 1997); Harding v. Dana Transport, Inc., 914 F. Supp. 1084, 1092-93 (D.N.J. 1996).

[20] See Worthington v. Endee, 177 F.R.D. 113, 118 (N.D.N.Y. 1998).

[21] Careful consideration must be given in situations where a CPA firm is retained as an outside consultant if that firm is also the provider's auditor. CPA firms that serve this dual role may be ethically proscribed from ignoring information learned during the investigation, thereby creating problems in preserving the privilege.

[22] This subsection only addresses the handling of employee interviews in the context of preserving the confidentiality of an internal investigation. See Chapter Five, for a complete discussion of the handling of employee interviews.

[23] The Justice Department's policy applies to all types of business organizations, including but not limited to corporations, partnerships, sole proprietorships, governmental entities and unincorporated associations.

[24] See Revised Principles at VI.

[25] See Id.

[26] See Id.

[27] In most cases, the Justice Department has indicated that it will not require a corporation to waive the attorney-client privilege with respect to legal advice concerning the government's criminal investigation. See Revised Principles at VI. n.3.

[28] See U.S.S.G. § 8C2.5(g).

[29] See In re Columbia/HCA Healthcare Corp., 192 F.R.D. 575 (M.D. Tenn. 2000) (forcing Columbia, a former target of a Justice Department investigation, to provide civil plaintiffs with documentation that Columbia had disclosed to the government).

Employee interviews

Introduction

One of the most dependable ways to determine facts in an internal investigation is through employee interviews. Employee interviews supply investigators not only with most of the relevant facts at issue, but also the context and rationale for many otherwise questionable practices. Review of the relevant documents is a necessary first step. By interviewing employees who created or handled the documents, or who have personal knowledge of relevant facts, one can come to understand whether there is an actual problem and, if so, the exact depth and scope of the problem.

This chapter gives practical pointers on how to conduct the interview process. It then discusses the criminal statutes that govern whether a person is obstructing justice, tampering with a witness, or engaging in retaliation. Finally, it discusses potential civil liability that can attach if the interview is not conducted in an appropriate manner.

Practical considerations

Employee interviews must be handled delicately. The interviewer must be able to quickly establish a rapport with the employee. He or she must ask questions that do not cause the employee to become defensive. The interviewer must be able to draw out as much relevant information as the employee possesses. Yet the interview must also ensure that the employee understands whom the interviewer is working for, as well as other important warnings. Through it all, the interviewer must tread carefully to avoid raising any questions as to witness tampering.

This section gives practical pointers to ensure that the interview is conducted in the best possible manner.

Interview methodology

You should avoid conducting interviews by yourself. From a legal standpoint, the second person will protect you from accusations that you acted inappropriately. From a practical standpoint, the second person will allow you to concentrate on the interview itself, instead of taking notes.

There are potential claims by the government (such as obstruction of justice and witness tampering) and potential claims by employees (such as harassment and false imprisonment) that are discussed later in this chapter. The potential for these claims to occur counsels strongly against conducting interviews without the presence and assistance of another person.

The importance of preparation and organization

Preparation and organization are crucial elements of an effective interview. Ideally, employee interviews should be scheduled after the relevant source documents have been reviewed. In addition, to the extent possible, prior to conducting any employee interviews the investigation team should prepare a chronology of events that contains information about the investigation, identi-fied by source. This chronology can then be updated after each interview. Ordering the internal investigation in this fashion will better place the employee's actions in the appropriate context, and put the interviewer in a position where he or she can ask more particular and meaningful questions. The interviewer should also have some understanding about the employee's possible biases and motives, prior to meeting the employee. This allows the interviewer to test the employee's recollection with regards to all relevant documents, as well as each issue in the case.

Before each interview, the interviewer should prepare an outline to establish a consistent line of questioning during the interview. Without an outline, or at the very least a list of subject areas, it is possible to miss reviewing areas about which the employee may have knowledge. "Winging it" is not advised, as unprepared interviewers are more likely to ask leading questions and are less able to appropriately react to new facts and unforeseen problems during the interview. Prepared interviewers, on the other hand, are more likely to ask questions that yield more relevant information, and they can better assess the employee's credibility and whether the employee would make a good grand jury or trial witness. Being prepared also helps avoid repeat interviews.

Scheduling employee interviews

The investigation team needs to take several factors into consideration when scheduling employee interviews. In many situations, speed is of the essence as the company is racing against government investigators. In these situations, it is preferable to interview those employees with the most information before the government does.

If time permits, employees should be interviewed in an order that minimizes the possibility of collusion or influence between or among employees. If the company suspects that senior-level management is involved in wrongdoing, the interviewer may opt to begin with interviews of lower-level employees and then work his or her way up the corporate ladder. By doing so, the interviewer is more likely to acquire all relevant information before conducting the most important and most sensitive interviews.

Establishing rapport

An employee will most likely be forthcoming and candid during the interview if he or she feels comfortable with the interviewer. Establishing rapport is key, and the dynamic between the interviewer and the employee may have a significant impact on the success of the interview. It is important to think seriously about which investigating attorney should conduct the interview. This may require choosing an attorney to conduct a particular interview based on his or her background, life experiences, interviewing style, and temperament.

The interviewing environment must be as non-threatening as possible— there should generally be no more than two members of the investigation team present for each employee interview. One attorney should ask questions while the other member of the investigation team takes copious notes and serves as a witness. Tracing notes is very important in the event that there is a dispute as to what was said during the interview. The company should schedule the interview at a time and location that is convenient for the employee, and should provide the employee with an approximation of how long the interview will last. The location should not expose the interview to casual observers—in other words, it should not be held where people walking by will become aware of the interview by observing it.

Several things can be done at the beginning of the interview to calm employee jitters. Begin with an introduction, a handshake, and an expression of appreciation for the employee's willingness to be interviewed. The interviewer's opening questions should give the employee an opportunity to share information about his or her background, experiences, and interests. By talking about such clearly non-threatening subjects, you can often establish a more informal atmosphere. The interview should focus on specific instances, not broad accusations. It is probably best for the interviewer to ask questions in a chronological fashion. He or she should obtain all of the necessary details about the events that occured within a chronological block of time before jumping to the next event. The interviewer should ask enough questions to ascertain the source of the employee's knowledge and distinguish between first-hand information, hearsay, and rumor.

The interviewer is well advised to not lose sight of the purpose of the inter-view, and to maintain his or her conduct accordingly. Although some employees may "crack" under the pressure of workplace interviews and admit wrongdoing, most do not. Investigating attorneys are not law enforcement officers; employee interviews should not resemble a police interrogation.

A non-confrontational and disarming approach is usually the more prudent approach. The interviewer should remain relaxed at all times and should not use a threatening or sarcastic tone, especially if he or she questions the employee's credibility. Any conduct that could be perceived as condescending (e.g., cutting the witness off) must be avoided. Interviewers should not highlight the weaknesses in the employee's narrative, as this can cause the employee to become defensive. If the interview becomes too confrontational or emotional, the interviewer should request a break. If the employee expresses a desire to end the interview, the interview should be terminated immediately.

Witnesses are more likely to respond favorably to open-ended, short, and simple questions. They appreciate lines of questioning that reflect that the interviewer has been paying attention to their testimony. When necessary, the interviewer may also have to appeal to a reluctant employee's sense of justice.

Although establishing rapport is important, the interviewer should not discuss his or her opinions or conclusions regarding the underlying facts in a misguided attempt to secure the employee's trust. This may tip the employee off as to the specifics of the investigation, or worse, distort the employee's testimony. The interviewer should also be aware of balancing the desire to investigate rumors with the desire not to spread unsubstantiated rumors. Sometimes, employees should be made aware that just because certain questions are asked, it does not mean that there is any substance behind those questions.

Toward the close of the interview, the employee should be given an opportunity to disclose any additional information or documents that he or she thinks the company might be interested in, and the names of persons with knowledge of the relevant events. The interview should close with the interviewer promising to call the employee with any follow-up questions, and with an open invitation to the employee to call the attorney with questions or subsequent recollections.

Establishing the attorney-client privilege and giving appropriate warnings

Investigators must structure employee interviews with the following four goals in mind:

1) Obtaining truthful information
2) Preserving the attorney-client privilege
3) Fulfilling their ethical obligations
4) Minimizing the interviewer's and the company's criminal and legal exposure during the investigation process

These goals can all be realized if the interviewer instructs the employee prior to conducting the interview about the interviewer's role and the employee's responsibilities. A company is well advised to distribute a checklist memo or script to all interviewing attorneys that directs them to ensure that the employee(s) being interviewed understand several important points.

First, it is essential that the employee understands that the interviewer is working on behalf of the company—not the employee. This establishes who the attorney-client privilege belongs to, and helps prevent later claims that the employee thought the attorney represented the employee instead of the company.[1]

Second, the interviewer must establish that the interview is being conducted within the bounds of the attorney-client privilege. Thus, the interviewers must tell the employee that the interview is privileged and confidential. The interviewer must also disclose that the privilege belongs to the company, not the employee, and that only the company can decide whether it wants to preserve the confidentiality of the interview or share this information. The company may decide to share the details of the investigation without the employee's consent or knowledge.

These important warnings stem in part from the American Bar Association (ABA) Model Rules of Professional Conduct. Model Rule 1.13[2] requires attorneys to avoid the representation of multiple clients within a company who may have conflicting interests. Failure to do so could result in disqualification from representing the company. Model Rule 4.3[3] makes clear that an interviewing attorney has an ethical obligation to explain that his/her loyalties are with the company, and not the employee. The attorney's failure to provide this explanation may possibly prevent the company from asserting or waiving the attorney-client privilege at a later point.[4] Given the Justice Department's increasing pressure on companies to waive the attorney-client privilege and work-product protection, no health care company can afford to share the attorney-client

privilege with any of its employees.[5] A proper warning will refute any notions of multiple representation.

To help establish the privilege, the interviewers may state that they have been asked by the company to investigate an allegation of questionable billing practices to provide legal advice to the company. They may further explain that in anticipation of litigation, they want to talk to the employee about matters within the scope of the employee's duties in order to provide the company with this legal advice.

Third, in certain interviews, it may be necessary to remind employees that they are required, as a condition of their employment, to cooperate and tell the truth. In other, rarer circumstances, it may also be necessary to warn employees that failure to do so can lead to demotion, suspension, reassignment, or termination.[6]

Fourth, to prevent rumors from flying and having future witnesses be forewarned, the interviewer should advise employees not tell anyone that they have been interviewed or share contents from the interview.

Fifth, the interviewer may also wish to reassure the employee that no retaliation will occur against the employee for cooperating with the investigation. The attorney must explain that it is illegal for anyone to retaliate against the employee for speaking to the government, and that he or she should call the interviewing attorney immediately in the event that he or she felt that this happened.

Finally, at the close of the interview, the employee should be instructed about his or her rights and responsibilities, should he or she be contacted by a government investigator. See sample memorandum to employees, attached Figure 4.3. The investigating attorney should tell the employee that government investigators 1) often try to reach potential witnesses in the evenings, weekends, or during times when witnesses are relaxed and would be most intimidated by a surprise call or visit; and 2) usually do not inform employees of their rights prior to interviewing them. The interviewer should give the employee numbers at which the interviewer can be contacted—even after business hours. In explaining the employee's rights, however, the interviewer must be sure not to give the impression that the company is instructing the employee not to cooperate with the government.

Although these warnings may engender a level of distrust and make it more difficult to obtain information, it is necessary to properly protect and control the information that is obtained during the interview.

Employee rights under **Weingarten**

In 1975, in *NLRB v. Weingarten*, the United States Supreme Court held that it was a violation of the National Labor Relations Act for an employer to conduct an investigation interview of a union employee if that employee "reasonably believe[d] that the interview [would] result in disciplinary action" and requested the presence of a union representative.[7] Twenty-five years later, the National Labor Relations Board (NLRB) reversed a 15-year precedent when it extended *Weingarten* to non-unionized employees in *Epilepsy Foundation of Northeast Ohio*.[8]

The *Weingarten* and *Epilepsy Foundation* decisions have imposed qualified requirements on health care companies that conduct investigation interviews. If a company fails to honor an employee's request and subsequently terminates the employee: 1) based on information obtained during the interview; or 2) for asserting, or attempting to assert, his or her *Weingarten* rights, the NLRB may reinstate the employee and award him or her back pay. A notice posting or other relief may also be granted whether or not reinstatement is ordered, if the company fails to honor the employee's legitimate *Weingarten* request.

Weingarten and *Epilepsy Foundation* are limited, however, to situations where the employee

1) actually requests to have a representative or co-worker present during the interview[9]

2) reasonably believes discipline may result from the interview.[10]

Health care companies are not obligated to inform employees of their *Weingarten* rights, and the employee's right does not extend to third persons, such as attorneys. The company may refuse to conduct the interview unless the employee is unaccompanied, and may take disciplinary action against the employee based on the results of the internal investigation, so long as this action does not stem from the employee's refusal to submit to an unaccompanied interview.[11] The company is not required to honor the employee's representative or co-worker selection if circumstances dictate precluding that individual, such as if the representative is a material witness[12] or if his or her unavailability would unduly delay the interview.[13]

An employee's exercise of his or her *Weingarten* rights may not "interfere with legitimate employer prerogatives."[14] Companies have "no duty to bargain with any union representative [or co-worker] who may be permitted to attend the investigation interview."[15] The individual cannot convert the interview into an adversary contest or a collective-bargaining confrontation; rather, his or her role is only to provide assistance and counsel to the employee being interviewed.[16] The company can insist on hearing the employee's first-hand account. The representative/co-worker is not allowed to interfere with the interview, and the company may need to discontinue the interview in certain limited circumstances.

In a *Weingarten* situation, health care companies have three options: 1) granting the employee's request and delaying the interview; 2) ending the interview completely; or 3) offering the employee the choice of continuing the interview unaccompanied, or being subject to discipline without an interview. Companies are urged to honor an employee's request to have a representative or co-worker present. If the employee's first choice is not available, the employee should be allowed to choose another representative or co-worker. At the beginning of the interview, the company should attempt to secure voluntary cooperation from the co-worker by instructing both the employee and the co-worker on the need to maintain the confidentiality of the interview.

Interview memoranda

Each health care company that decides to initiate an investigation must, at the beginning of that investigation, weigh the benefits and consequences of creating records of employee interviews, and develop a structure and plan for the recording of employee interviews accordingly. A company (in consultation with its outside counsel) should adopt a policy for drafting interview memos and handling interview notes, with the understanding that this information may be distributed to the government at a later date. Indeed, as discussed in Chapter 4, the Department of Justice often strongly requests that companies hand over attorney work-product materials. This decision will affect how employee interviews are conducted and whether interview memos will be created.

If it is decided that an interview memo should be created, it should be drafted shortly after the employee interview has been conducted. There are two ways to go about drafting an interview memo. The first way is to write the memorandum as a dry statement, summarizing the employee's interview. The second way is to include a great deal of attorney opinion work product scattered throughout. Both methods, and the advantages and disadvantages of each, are discussed below.

Prefatory language in both kinds of interview memos can help ensure that the attorney-client privilege and work-product protection are not waived. All interview memos must be clearly marked with a readily identifiable legend at the top of each page that reads, **"PRIVILEGED AND CONFIDENTIAL ATTORNEY-CLIENT/WORK PRODUCT. DO NOT DUPLICATE. DO NOT DISSEMINATE."** The interview memos should also contain a preamble that confirms that the investigating attorney took certain precautionary measures prior to obtaining information from the employee. This preamble should indicate that 1) the employee interview was conducted for purposes of rendering legal advice to the company 2) necessary warnings were given to the employee at the onset of the interview 3) the employee understood the warnings and agreed to continue with the interview 4) the employee agreed to keep the interview confidential; and 5) the employee did not review the interview memo, nor certify a statement confirming the accuracy of the interview memorandum. If the interview was preliminary, this too should be reflected in the memo.

Both kinds of memos should objectively describe the employee's responses to the questions. They should state the date, start and end time, and location of the interview, as well as the names of persons who were present for the interview. The memos should be devoid of speculation, generalizations, unrelated observations, and conclusions that are not supported by evidence.

In writing the first kind of memo, the interviewer should stick to factual matters only—what the employee said in response to questions. There should be no commentary and no analysis from the attorney. If this memo is ultimately given to the government, the only work-product it will necessarily reveal are subject areas and particular questions that were of interest to the attorney.

In the second kind of memo, the attorney's opinion work-product (which is protected) should be included in the text so that a good-faith argument can be made, if necessary, that the memo is not discoverable. Although it is important that the interview memo be as precise as possible, it must be more than a recitation of the employee's statement. The interviewer may set forth the disputed and undisputed facts, and possible areas for further investigation. he or she may give a detailed assessment of the employee's credibility and testimony, level of evasiveness or nervousness, and whether the employee gave contradictory statements. It cannot be a verbatim record of the interview, which may be difficult to protect as attorney work-product.[17]

The advantages of the first method—only factual statements—are increasing in light of the Department of Justice's policy in asking corporations to waive certain work-product protection. The government is most interested in the substance of the interviews—what the employee said when first questioned. By writing memos that stick to the facts, the company can hand over material without jeopardizing more sensitive attorney opinion work-product and attorney advice to the client.

Use of investigators

The company should also consider using investigators as part of the interviewing process. Investigators can be extremely helpful in several respects. First, an investigator's participation in interviews can defuse later disputes in those cases where conflicting "memories" of what was said arise. Using the investigator as a witness to the conversation avoids counsel's role as a material witness (and the concomitant friction regarding the rules of professional responsibility) in the event of subsequent legal proceedings.

Investigators may also bring to bear their specialized skills and training in gathering certain types of information. For example, they may be adept at database searches or other sophisticated investigative techniques unfamiliar to a lawyer. Investigators may also be used in pre-textual matters to gather information from otherwise uncooperative sources.

Finally, an organization's counsel should consider the economies of hiring outside investigators. An investigator's comprehensive techniques and efficiency may save valuable time and money in the end.

Avoiding criminal liability

A company's reputation can suffer from allegations that it engaged in witness tampering during its handling of an internal investigation. This risk must be avoided at all costs. At the beginning of an investigation, all members of the investigation team should receive instructions on the breadth and depth of the federal obstruction of justice and subornation of perjury statutes, and the applicability of these statutes to employee interviews. This will put the investigating team on notice that the law places limits on their interactions with potential witnesses.

Obstruction of justice

The principal federal obstruction of justice statutes that health care companies conducting employee interviews need be concerned about are as follows:

- 18 U.S.C. § 1503 (the general obstruction of justice statute)
- 18 U.S.C. §§ 1512-1515 (the tampering provisions of the Victim and Witness Protection Act)

- 18 U.S.C. § 1505 (the obstruction of proceedings for department agencies and committees)
- 18 U.S.C. § 1519 (the Sarbanes-Oxley Act's destruction-of-records statute)[18]
- 18 U.S.C. § 1518 (Obstruction of Criminal Investigation of Healthcare Offenses
- 18 U.S.C. § 1516 (the obstruction of federal audit)

These statutes prohibit witness tampering, and make it a felony to engage in misleading conduct to influence the testimony of another person in an official proceeding.

Conducting attorney interviews can run afoul of one or more of these statutes if they discourage employees from cooperating with government investigators. They must avoid any statements or comments that could be construed as an attempt to mislead or influence witnesses. Attorneys should not characterize the company's position or summarize the testimony of other witnesses in their interactions with potential witnesses. At the close of the interview, the investigating attorney should restate the employee's rights (including his or her right to speak to government investigators), and the importance of truthfully answering all questions posed by government investigators if they decide to give an interview.

The general statute on obstruction of justice

The basic federal statute on obstruction of justice is found at 18 U.S.C. § 1503. It prohibits "corruptly or by threats or force, or by any threatening letter or communication … influenc[ing], obstruct[ing], or imped[ing], or endeavor[ing] to influence, obstruct, or impede, the due administration of justice" in a pending judicial proceeding. This catch-all language allows for the prosecution of acts that are not prohibited by other obstruction statutes.

Section 1503 requires that a judicial proceeding be pending.[19] The statute does not proscribe conduct that takes place wholly outside the context of an ongoing judicial or quasi-judicial proceeding.[20] Courts have generally avoided adopting a bright-line rule as to when a judicial proceeding is pending, but consider such a proceeding to be pending once a grand jury becomes actively engaged or a complaint has been filed in civil litigation.[21] The grand jury need not hear actual testimony, and no subpoenas need have been issued, for Section 1503 to apply.[22] Obstruction of an investigation conducted by the Customs Service, Internal Revenue Service, FBI, or some other governmental agency that is not connected to a grand jury investigation will not, however, constitute a "judicial proceeding."[23]

A person accused of violating the general obstruction statute must have knowledge, notice, or information of the pending status with regard to the judicial proceeding.[24] Although the courts generally agree that Section 1503 requires a showing of specific intent, they differ in the interpretation of that term. Courts do allow, however, a defendant's corrupt intent or motive to be inferred from his conduct and his presumed knowledge of the natural, foreseeable consequences of his actions.[25]

Obstruction of proceedings for department agencies and committees

Federal statute 18 U.S.C. § 1505 sets forth the same requirements as the general obstruction of justice statute, and contains a similarly worded catch-all clause. Construction of Section 1505's knowledge and specific intent requirements can be used to inform construction of Section 1503's, and vice versa. Section 1505 differs from Section 1503 in that it relates to administrative proceedings pending before a federal agency or department, or Congress, as opposed to judicial proceedings. Courts have also broadened the scope of Section 1505 to include investigations conducted by government agencies that have both investigative and adjudicative powers, such as the NLRB,[26] the Immigration and Naturalization Service, and the Internal Revenue Service.[27]

The Victim and Witness Protection Act

The primary purpose of the Victim and Witness Protection Act (VWPA) of 1982 was to protect victims, witnesses, and informants from persons who act upon them in order to obstruct justice. It has become the predominant obstruction of justice statute since its enactment. The government must prove the following four elements to obtain a conviction under the VWPA—that the defendant 1) knowingly 2) engaged in intimidation, physical force, threats, misleading conduct, or corrupt persuasion towards another person 3) with the intent to influence, delay, or prevent testimony, or to cause that person to withhold evidence or testimony 4) from an official proceeding.

The VWPA differs from Sections 1503 and 1505 in several important ways. First, it defines "official proceeding"[29] more broadly than Sections 1303 and 1305. Second, the VWPA does not require that the official proceeding be pending or about to be instituted,[30] or that the defendant was aware that the official proceeding was pending.[31] The most striking difference between Sections 1503 and 1505, on one hand, and the VWPA on the other hand, relates to the element of intent. Although Section 1512 appears on the surface to require that the defendant acted corruptly, the circuits are split on whether the meaning of Section 1512's "corruptly persuades" requires more than a showing of an improper motive.[32]

Obstruction of criminal investigations of health care offenses

When Congress passed the Health Insurance Portability and Accountability Act of 1996 (HIPAA), it included a provision aimed specifically at obstruction of criminal investigations of health care offenses. See 18 U.S.C. § 1518. Like the general obstruction statute, this statute requires the government to prove that the person acted corruptly or by threat of force. It prohibits conduct that endeavors to influence, intimidate, or impede any witness, or which willfully prevents, obstructs, misleads, or delays the communication to a criminal investigator of information relating to a federal health care offense. It carries a maximum fine (not specificied in the U.S. Code) and maximum jail time of five years.

Obstruction of a federal audit

Federal statute 18 U.S.C. § 1516, the obstruction of federal audit statute, makes it a felony offense to influence, obstruct, or impede a federal auditor who is auditing a person, entity, or program that receives $100,000 or more from the federal government "in any one-year period." The statute requires a showing that the defendant acted with an "intent to deceive or defraud."

Subornation of perjury

Interviewing attorneys must also conduct employee interviews in a circumspect manner to avoid any accusations that they suborned perjury. 18 U.S.C. § 1622, the federal subornation of perjury statute, forbids "procur[ing] another to commit any perjury." All inducements and instigations of perjury are illegal.

Retaliation

The Sarbanes-Oxley Act (SO Act), as discussed in Chapter Eight, prohibits companies from making adverse employment decisions against employees who provide truthful information to law enforcement officers "relating to the commission or possible commission" of a federal offense, or who have commenced or participated in an investigation or proceeding relating to an alleged violation of federal law. Companies that conduct investigations should adopt investigation policies that do not abridge the SO Act, in order to avoid running afoul of federal law when dealing with such employees. Engaging in unlawful retaliatory conduct could result in both individual and corporate liability. No adverse employment decision should be made regarding these employees unless it can be demonstrated by clear and convincing evidence that the company would have taken the adverse employment action irrespective of any protected activity taken by the employee.

Avoiding civil liability

Hasty, incomplete, or improperly conducted employee interviews can substantially increase a health care company's civil liability. Employees who feel wrongly accused or maligned by a workplace interview have legal weapons against their employer, even if they are not disciplined as a result of the interview. These legal challenges usually utilize one of a handful of tort theories: intentional infliction of emotional distress, invasion of privacy, defamation, or false imprisonment.

Employee interviews that are conducted in a generally reasonable manner normally do not result in liability. Although civil liability usually attaches only to highly egregious conduct, companies should be mindful of how they handle employee interviews because courts, when reviewing employee tort claims, will take into consideration the length of the interview, the employer's conduct during the interview, and whether the employer had a good faith belief that the employee had engaged in improper conduct.

Invasion of privacy

There are four common law theories under which an employee can bring an invasion of privacy claim: 1) intrusion into the employee's seclusion, solitude, or private affairs; 2) appropriation of the employee's likeness for the employer's advantage; 3) public disclosure of private facts about the employee; and 4) publicity that places the employee in a false light.

When deciding an "intrusion upon seclusion" claim, courts will consider whether the following four criteria exist:

1) The intrusion was reasonable

2) The employer's actions would have been highly offensive to the average reasonable person

3) The employee's conduct being questioned was objectively or subjectively a private affair

4) The company had a legitimate reason for its conduct[33]

The employee must also demonstrate that the employer's action would have caused mental suffering, shame, or humiliation to a reasonable person.

Health care companies can reduce their potential tort liability under an "intrusion upon seclusion" claim by stating in a published personnel policy that they expressly reserve the right to interview employees regarding workplace misconduct, and that refusal to cooperate could result in discipline, including termination. Employees should be required to sign an acknowledgement form regarding this policy. Companies can generally avoid liability under this claim by avoiding delving into employees' private matters unnecessarily (e.g., off-duty activities or romantic life), and by maintaining the confidentiality of these interviews. All interview memos should reflect the focus of the interview and the interviewer's reasonable conduct.

Intentional infliction of emotional distress

An employee may bring a tort claim for intentional infliction of emotional distress based on an abusive and intimidating interview. For this claim to be successful, the employee must demonstrate that the employer intentionally or recklessly engaged in conduct that was "so outrageous in character and extreme in degree as to go beyond all bounds of decency, and to be regarded as atrocious and utterly intolerable in a civilized community."[34] The employee must also show that the employer's conduct caused severe emotional distress or physical harm.

When determining whether the employer's conduct is actionable, a court will consider the length of the interview, the employer's conduct during the interview, whether the employer had a good-faith belief that the employee had engaged in improper conduct, and whether the employee was hostile or unreasonable during the interview. Defenses to the claim include the absence of outrageous conduct,[35] privilege, and the exclusivity of workers' compensation remedies.

Defamation

Employees have also sued employers for defamation based on careless investigative procedures. In order to successfully bring a defamation claim, the employee must establish that: 1) a defamatory statement was maliciously made about the employee, and 2) this statement was published to a third party who understood that it referred to the employee.[36] If the defamatory statement was not maliciously made, no cause of action will be found.[37] Companies that share the statement only on a "need-to-know-basis" are also protected by a qualified privilege.[38]

False imprisonment

Employees who are detained or restrained without their consent during an interview may sue their employer for false imprisonment. The restraint does not need to be physical to be actionable; it can be the result of physical or mental intimidation.

Most states permit employers to interview employees for a reasonable amount of time and in a reasonable manner, so long as the interview is supported by a legitimate business interest. Companies may also avoid the "confinement" element of the false imprisonment tort by giving the employee the option of cooperating in an investigation interview.[39]

[1] See, e.g., United States v. Aramony, 88 F. 3d 1369, 1389-92 (4th Cir. 1996) (former CEO of United Way claimed that attorney representing the organization in an internal investigation also represented him personally). Distributing a checklist memorandum will bolster the company's contention that interviewed employees were fully informed of their rights and responsibilities during the internal investigation and that company attorneys acted within the bounds of the law.

[2] Model Rule 1.13 imposes an ethical obligation on the investigating attorney to state that the client is the company when it is apparent that the company's interests are adverse to the employee.

[3] Model Rule 4.3 provides that "[w]hen the lawyer knows or reasonably should know that the unrepresented person misunderstands the lawyer's role in the matter, the lawyer shall make reasonable efforts to correct the misunderstanding."

[4] See, e.g., United States v. Hart, 1992 U.S. Dist. LEXIS 17796 (E.D. La. Nov. 16, 1992) (communications between investigating attorney and interviewed employee were protected when attorney never identified herself as solely representing the company). But see, e.g., United States v. International Bhd. of Teamsters, 119 F.3d 210, 215-16 (2d Cir. 1997) (employee's "reasonable belief" that he was represented by investigating attorney not sufficient to assert privilege).

[5] See Chapter Four for a discussion of the Justice Department's Principles of Federal Prosecution of Business Organizations.

[6] See, e.g., United States v. Sawyer, 878 F. Supp. 295, 296 (D. Mass. 1995) (employee had obligation to assist in-house counsel with company internal investigation). A company's ability to terminate an employee who refuses to be interviewed depends on the employee's employment rights, the state law involved, and the specific circumstances of each case.

[7] NLRB v. Weingarten, 420 U.S. 251 (1975).

[8] Epilepsy Foundation of Northeast Ohio, 331 NLRB 676 (2000).

[9] See Weingarten, 420 U.S. at 257.

[10] See id. at 257n.5.

[11] See id. at 258-59.

[12] See, e.g., Federal Prison System, 25 F.L.R.A. 210, 228 (1987) (company legitimately excluded requested co-worker who was part of investigation until co-worker's interview was completed).

[13] See, e.g., Pac. Gas & Elec. Co., 253 N.L.R.B. 1143, 1151 (1981) (exclusion of first choice justified when requested co-worker was located 20 minutes away); N.J. Bell Tel. Co., 308 N.L.R.B. 277, 280

(1992) (company had legitimate interest in excluding requested co-worker who had been ejected and escorted from a prior inquiry).

[14] See Weingarten, 420 U.S. at 258.

[15] Id. at 259.

[16] Id. at 263.

[17] Employee interviews should not be taped or videotaped for this very reason.

[18] See Chapter Eight for a discussion of Sarbanes-Oxley's statute on obstruction of justice.

[19] See, e.g., United States v. Vesich, 724 F.2d 451 (5th Cir. 1984).

[20] See, e.g., United States v. Brown, 688 F.2d 596 (9th Cir. 1982) (Section 1503 not applicable to defendant who attempted to prevent seizure of narcotics by thwarting target of valid search warrant).

[21] See, e.g., United States. v. Monus, 128 F.3d 376 (6th Cir. 1997) (finding pending judicial proceeding based on investigation by IRS agent working closely with grand jury); United States v. Lundwall, 1 F. Supp. 2d 249 (S.D.N.Y. 1998) (pendency of civil action satisfies Section 1505's "pending proceeding" requirement).

[22] See, e.g., United States v. Walasek, 527 F.2d 676 (3d Cir. 1975) (grand jury need not hear actual testimony for proceeding to be considered pending); United States v. Gravely, 840 F.2d 1156 (4th Cir. 1988) (Section 1503 violated with destruction of documents when defendant was aware that grand jury would likely seek destroyed documents).

[23] See, e.g., United States v. Tham, 960 F.2d 1391 (9th Cir. 1991) (Section 1503 pertains only to acts that thwart government's judicial functions).

[24] Knowledge of the pendency of the judicial proceeding differs from knowledge of a federal investigation. See, e.g., United States v. Davis, 183 F.3d 231 (3d Cir. 1999) (distinguishing between knowledge of federal investigation and knowledge of grand jury investigation).

[25] See, e.g., United States v. Silverman, 745 F.2d 1386, 1393 (11th Cir. 1984).

[26] See, e.g., Rice v. United States, 356 F.2d 709 (8th Cir. 1966).

[27] See, e.g., United States v. Abrams, 427 F.2d 86 (2d Cir. 1970).

[28] See, e.g., United States v. Lewis, 657 F.2d 44 (4th Cir. 1981).

[29] 18 U.S.C. § 1515(a)(1) defines "official proceeding" as a proceeding before: 1) a federal judge, magistrate, or grand jury; 2) Congress; 3) an authorized federal agency; or 4) before an insurance regulatory agency involving insurance activities that affect interstate commerce.

[30] Although the obstructive conduct must be in connection with an official proceeding, Section 1512 also covers obstructive conduct when the defendant expected that an official proceeding would be initiated in the foreseeable future.

[31] See, e.g., United States v. Frankhauser, 80 F.3d 641 (1st Cir. 1996).

[32] See United States v. Davis, 183 F.3d 231 (3d Cir. 1999) ("corruptly persuades" requires more than an improper motive, for the purpose of obstructing justice); but cf. United States v. Thompson, 76 F.3d 442 (2d Cir. 1996) ("corruptly persuades" requires only an improper purpose).

[33] *See Restatement (Second) of Torts, § 652B (1977).*

[34] *See Restatement (Second) of Torts, § 46(1) cmt (d) (1976).*

[35] *See, e.g.,* Wenzer v. Consolidated Rail Corp., *464 F. Supp. 643, 650 (E.D. Pa), aff'd., 612 F.2d 576 (3d Cir. 1979).*

[36] *See, e.g., Quinones v. United States, 492 F.2d 1269, 1274-75 (3d Cir. 1974).*

[37] *See, e.g., Vackar v. Packages Machinery Co., 841 F. Supp. 310, 314 (N.D. Cal. 1993).*

[38] *See, e.g.,* Smith v. Bell Atlantic Network Services, *1995 WL 389697, * 5 (E.D. Pa. June 28, 1995) (employees who made no defamatory statements outside of the scope of their investigatory duties were protected by a conditional privilege).*

[39] *See, e.g., id. (noting that room was unlocked and that employee, who was not physically restrained, never asked to leave interview).*

Disclosure of overpayments—What do you do if you find a compliance problem?

If the internal investigation identifies areas of concern, the provider should undertake remedial steps to ensure that any compliance issues are resolved going forward. This may involve additional training of employees and staff, preparation or amendment of polices and procedures, institution of checks and cross checks, reprimands, or terminations of malfeasing employees.

The provider may decide to limit its response to those internal compliance efforts and to take no further action, assuming that it is not under any legal obligation to disclose its findings. The nature and source of an obligation to disclose is discussed below and in Chapter Eight on the Sarbanes-Oxley Act. But even if the law does not expressly obligate a provider to disclose its findings, good compliance practice dictates that the provider should at least consider whether the results of an internal investigation should be disclosed to a fiscal intermediary, a governmental agency, or even a private payor. We discuss balancing the benefits and risks of voluntary disclosure below.

Is a provider required to voluntarily disclose the results of its internal investigation?

When properly protected under attorney-client privilege, the results of most internal investigations do not have to be disclosed. Absent a specific duty to disclose, corporations are not legally required to report past wrongdoing to the government. However, where the internal investigation discloses an overpayment, there is some controversy about what actions a provider must take.

The Office of Inspector General (OIG) clearly views the Social Security Act (SSA) as imposing on providers the obligation to disclose when they have been overpaid by a government program and, beyond that, to repay the amounts paid in error. However, the legal authority for that position is not clear. In its *Compliance Program Guidance for Hospitals*, the OIG interprets the SSA to require providers to disclose overpayment. The Medicare fraud and abuse provision, 42 U.S.C. § 1320a-7b(a)(3) provides: Whoever—

> (3) having knowledge of the occurrence of any event affecting (A) his initial or continued right to any such benefit or payment, ... conceals or fails to disclose such event with an intent fraudulently to secure such benefit or payment either in a greater amount or quantity than is due or when no such benefit or payment is authorized, shall (i) in the case of such a statement, representation, concealment, failure, or conversion by any person in connection with the furnishing (by that person) of items or services for which payment is or may be made under the program, be guilty of a felony and upon conviction thereof fined not more than $25,000 or imprisoned for not more than five years or both ...

See *OIG Compliance Program Guidance for Hospitals*, 63 *Fed. Reg.* 8789 (1998). However, the above provision does not expressly address overpayments, and certainly not restitution of the amounts overpaid. Some legal pundits question whether a provider's discovery of an overpayment is an "event" as contemplated in that provision. However, it is clear that the government's position is that funds improperly paid cannot be retained without penalty.

In 2002, the Centers for Medicare and Medicaid Services (CMS) proposed a rule making the disclosure of "known" overpayments mandatory.[1] The proposed rule would require a provider that has "identified" a Medicare overpayment to return the money within 60 days. The proposed rule also requires the provider to present a written explanation of the reason for the overpayment. The rule applies to "known" overpayments. Thus, if the rule is finalized as anticipated, a provider with notice of an overpayment may need to conduct at least a limited internal investigation to determine whether the duty to disclose has been triggered. The fact that this regulation has not been finalized raises the question: If the obligation is clear, why not finalize the rule? Nevertheless, the question remains open.

How do I determine whether I have a "known" overpayment?

The proposed regulation above expressly applies to "known" overpayments. Given the complexity of Medicare rules and regulations, there may be a good faith uncertainty over the appropriateness of certain claims and, thus, whether there is a "known" overpayment. Where it is not clear that a claim is erroneous, some providers take the position that, until the government makes an overpayment determination or there is legal advice to resolve the ambiguity, they will have no obligation to determine the existence of one.[2]

An internal investigation may reveal illegal behavior that does not result in an overpayment, such as a kickback scheme (42 U.S.C. § 1320a-7b). Arguably, there is no overpayment, so the admonition to return overpayments does not drive the disclosure issue. In that case, the Fifth Amendment protection from self-incrimination might be seen as protecting any individual from an obligation to self-disclose. However, corporations and other fictitious persona are not protected by the Fifth Amendment. Moreover, some prosecutors have argued that funds received in an unlawful kickback exchange may involve false claims and thus overpayments. See *U.S. v. Kensington Hospital*, 760 F. Supp. 1120 (E.D. PA. 1991). *U.S. ex rel Thompson v. Columbia HCA*, 20 F. Supp 2d 1017 (S.D. Tex. 1996). Thus, careful consideration must be given to disclosures.

Voluntary disclosure of overpayments may be required under the terms of an existing corporate integrity agreement (CIA). Most settlements under the False Claims Act, or with the OIG alone, result in the provider's agreeing to a CIA. The typical CIA requires a provider to put compliance measures in place to ensure the integrity of federal health care program claims submitted by the provider. Such measures generally include requirements to: (1) hire a compliance officer and appoint a compliance committee; (2) develop written standards and policies; (3) conduct an employee training program; (4) audit billings to federal health care programs; (5) establish a hotline; (6) restrict employment of excluded individuals; and (7) submit a variety of reports to the OIG. Most significantly, guidance on CIAs published in 2000 makes clear that the CIA imposes express obligations on providers to report overpayments. The risk of failing to comply with the CIA is that the settlement agreement will be violated, and the provider may once again be subject to prosecution for the claims settled. See "Frequently Asked Questions Related to OIG CIAs," Office of Inspector General, *Compliance Guidance*, Nov. 6, 2000.[3]

Advantages and disadvantages of voluntary disclosure

When voluntary disclosure is not an obligation but an option, the provider may encounter diverse opinions among its decision-makers. Some may express a desire to bring the potential problem to the attention of the government and attempt to seek a resolution of the matter—quickly, and without incurring criminal penalties, civil fines, or exclusions. On the other hand, some decision-makers might prefer not to draw the scrutiny of an enforcement agency, reasoning that the risks of that scrutiny outweigh the potential positives. The decision about whether to disclose an issue requires a complex analysis of all the facts and circumstances, and a balancing of the benefits and risks.

Advantages of voluntary disclosure

The simple benefit of a voluntary disclosure and repayment is that the provider is returning money to which it was not entitled. Providers may be motivated by good citizenship to self-disclose a problem in the provider organization. However, while confession may be good for the soul, the advantages of voluntary disclosure are more often measured by comparison to having the problem discovered, investigated, and prosecuted by an enforcement authority.

Provider controls the message

A self-disclosure involves providing a narrative that will identify the overpayment and possible explanation of the error that caused it. To voluntarily disclose billing problems, the provider should draft a document that casts the provider in the most favorable light. That is, the provider can describe the issue in a non-adversarial context, asserting defenses and noting mitigating circumstances. In calculating amounts due, a provider can propose to net any underpayments it learns of through investigation, against the overpayment determination.

If the law is vague, the provider can highlight the ambiguity, and describe alternate interpretations. The narrative should avoid legal conclusions (such as that the claims were "false" or that the billing agent "knew" the claims were wrong) and admissions against its interest. The provider can note the corrective actions taken since discovery. The provider can also control the time, manner, and circumstance of the disclosure. Compared to receiving a subpoena, search warrant, notice of an audit, or visits from program integrity officers, the voluntary disclosure has obvious advantages when the provider controls the message.

Limits further inquiry and enforcement

By voluntarily disclosing the mistake, the provider may persuade the government to forego any enforcement actions beyond the repayment. This is true especially where an overpayment is repaid and appropriate compliance efforts have been undertaken (e.g., remedial trainee, dismissal of the wrongdoers, or the incorporation of new control mechanisms).[4] See June 3, 1998 memoradum to all United States Attorneys from Eric H. Holder, Jr., Deputy Attorney General, re Guidance on the Use of the False Claims Act in Civil Health Care Matters.

Improves the chances of avoiding a corporate integrity agreement

By bringing the problem to the attention of the OIG, the provider may earn considerable credibility. The organization's investigative report and the related statement of program losses may be relied upon by the OIG in verifying the disclosed information and reporting the matter. Voluntary disclosure may thereby prevent a disruptive outside investigation, and expensive and time-consuming litigation by the enforcement agency. If an outside inquiry cannot be avoided entirely, the disclosure may either avoid, or allow, negotiation of the scope of the government's investigation and interviews of employees. The disclosure may enable the provider to avoid discovery battles both as to content and timing of production.

In the event that the government goes forward with an enforcement action based on the voluntary disclosure, the disclosing party may nonetheless receive more favorable treatment than it would otherwise receive. For example, a CIA may not be required if a matter is settled based on a self-disclosure. In an "Open Letter to Health Care Providers," November 20, 2001, the OIG modified the policies applicable in civil settlement processes, including CIAs:

> We also recognize that in certain cases it may be appropriate to release the OIG's administrative exclusion authorities without a corporate integrity agreement. I have directed my staff to consider the following criteria when determining whether to require a corporate integrity agreement, and, if so, the substance of that agreement: (1) whether the provider self-disclosed the alleged misconduct ...

Similarly, the OIG has published non-binding guidelines to be used in assessing whether the permissive exclusion should be imposed on a provider. See "Criteria for Implementing Permissive Exclusion Authority Under Section 1128(b)(7) of the [SSA]," 62 FR 67,392 (1997). These guidelines identify specific factors and explain how they would be used by the OIG to assess a permissive exclusion decision. The OIG's criteria include the general category of "Defendant's Response to Allegations/Determination of Unlawful Conduct" and within that category lists the following:

> 6. B. Did the defendant bring the activity in question to the attention of the appropriate government officials prior to any government action, e.g., was there any voluntary disclosure regarding the alleged wrongful conduct?

Reduces fines and penalties

In return for voluntary submission of information that documents wrongdoing, the provider may seek to resolve the improper billing issue by repaying the amount improperly paid. By saving the government the cost of investigation, the provider may incur a smaller penalty compared to what the government could have sought had the settlement been the result of the government's own investigation.

The disclosure gives the provider a reasonable chance to mitigate fines and penalties. Under the False Claims Act, 31 U.S.C. § 3729, a disclosure within 30 days from the date on which the defendant first obtains information on the violation will reduce exposure to fines. Instead of triple damages, the (Department of Justice) DOJ is limited to double damages.

Similarly, U.S. Sentencing Commission Guidelines Manual, § 5K2. 16, *Voluntary Disclosure of Offense* (policy statement) provides that if the defendant voluntarily discloses to authorities the existence of, and accepts responsibility for, the offense prior to the discovery of such offense, "a departure below the applicable sentencing guideline range for that offense may be warranted."

In addition, in determining the culpability score of an organization (and therefore the fine amount), the Sentencing Guidelines provide a large incentive to those organizations that self-report. If an organization self-reports (1) "prior to an imminent threat of disclosure or government investigation" and (2) "within a reasonably prompt time after becoming aware of the offense," the organization can subtract five points from its culpability score. U.S.S.G. § 8C 2.5(g). Those five points can cut in half the fine amount that the organization is exposure to. Moreover, for an organization to get credit under the guidelines for having an effective compliance program, it must not "unreasonably delay" reporting the offense to the government. U.S.S.G. § 8C 2.5(f).

Disadvantages of voluntary disclosure

Although the advantages of voluntary disclosure are measured against the assumption that the government will learn of the errors through sources other than self-disclosure, the disadvantages are measured against the assumption that, absent the disclosure, the matter will be disclosed by a third party (e.g., by a fiscal intermediary or by the competition) to an enforcement agency by a *qui tam* action.

There are no guarantees that the provider will get a break

There are no guarantees that voluntary disclosure will result in a decision by the government to refrain from proceeding criminally or civilly against the provider. Although the provider might be credited for its compliance efforts to some extent, the provider could remain subject to potential liability based on its failure to prevent the illegal or excess payments.

There will be an overpayment to be repaid

In short, the voluntary disclosure does not come without a literal cost.

There is no guarantee that the government will view the issue as the provider views it

The government may not be satisfied that the provider's internal investigation has uncovered the entire scope of the problem. Once the government is involved, it might find bigger problems than were anticipated at the time of self-disclosure. The government may view the problem very differently from the provider, and may impose fines substantially in excess of what the provider believes is appropriate.

There is no guarantee that the government will accept the provider's compliance plan

The government may view the client's compliance efforts as insufficient, and may impose new and expensive compliance obligations.

The provider may waive certain privileges

The client may be asked to waive certain privileges as part of its voluntary disclosure. See *In re: Columbia/HCA Healthcare Corp. Billing Practices Litigation*, (293 f.3d 289, 6th Cir. 2002). The Sixth Circuit held that a health care provider could not assert the attorney-client or work-product protections against private-party plaintiff lawsuits, after having entered a selective waiver agreement in a preceding case with the government. The agreement with the government called for the release of internal billing audits to the government in exchange for protection of the provider's privileges in subsequent cases. However, the Sixth Circuit found that the agreement was invalid as to subsequent civil litigation because the privileges do not allow selective waiver. The court ruled that once a party has waived the privilege by disclosure to a third party, the privilege may not be re-asserted as to the covered information. See Chapter Four, "Preserving attorney-client privilege and work-product protection."

Where does a provider disclose?

In the event the provider ultimately decides to proceed with a voluntary disclosure, it will have several avenues when it comes to disclosing areas of non-compliance. These choices include:

Fiscal intermediaries or carriers. Matters that involve billing errors can generally be disclosed to the fiscal intermediary or carrier that processes claims and issues payment on behalf of the government agency responsible for the particular federal health care program (e.g., CMS for matters involving Medicare). The program contractors are responsible for processing the refund, and will review the circumstances surrounding the initial overpayment. A provider may also choose to go directly to CMS, at either a regional office or the main CMS office. (A provider may opt for this choice if the fiscal intermediary is considered to be too strict in its interpretation of a provision, or if fiscal intermediary auditors are considered to be too confrontational.)

It must be noted that a voluntary disclosure to the fiscal intermediary may not stop all inquiry. When a provider returns an overpayment equal to or greater than 20 percent of the total annual Medicare payments for that provider, (or in any other circumstances in which there are suspected patterns of inappropriate payment), the contractor is directed to perform data analysis for patterns of inappropriate program payment and possibly report the matter to the OIG.[5]

Law Enforcement. If the investigation reveals matters that, in the provider's reasonable assessment, potentially violate federal criminal, civil, or administrative laws, the provider, through counsel, may bring the matter to the attention of the Department of Justice (DOJ), most often through a local U. S. Attorney's Office. The DOJ has prosecutorial discretion over federal criminal statutes and regulations and the False Claims Act (FCA). For matters involving Medicaid or state-funded programs, the provider may consider a state attorney general.

Office of Inspector General. The OIG has authority over the imposition of civil monetary penalties and exclusions. Commonly, a provider will make a same-time disclosure to both the OIG and the DOJ.

Voluntary disclosure protocol

The Inspector General has developed a formal voluntary disclosure program for Medicare and Medicaid issues. This self-disclosure protocol sets out specific steps, including a detailed audit methodology, that may be undertaken if the provider wishes to work openly and cooperatively with the OIG on a voluntary disclosure. Because a provider's disclosure can involve anything from a simple error to outright fraud, the OIG does not make firm commitments as to any specific benefit to the disclosing entity. The protocol can help a health care provider initiate a dialogue with the OIG. However, the OIG is not bound by any findings made by the disclosing provider, and is not obligated to resolve the matter in any particular manner.

Upon review of the provider's disclosure submission, the OIG may conclude that the disclosed matter nonetheless warrants a referral to the DOJ or other government agencies affected by that matter. Alternatively, the provider may request the participation of a representative of the DOJ or a local United

States Attorney's Office in settlement discussions, in order to get a global settlement to resolve potential liability under the FCA or other laws.

To participate, the disclosing provider will be expected to submit a written narrative that covers very specific elements. The OIG requests access to all audit work papers without the assertion of privileges or limitations on the information produced. In the normal course of verification, the OIG will not request production of written communications subject to the attorney-client privilege. However, the provider may be asked to waive that privilege. The health care provider must conduct an internal financial assessment to estimate the monetary impact of the disclosed matter, and must submit to the OIG a certification stating that, to the best of the individual's knowledge, the report contains truthful information and is based on a good faith effort to assist the OIG in its inquiry of the disclosed matter.

Upon receipt of a health care provider's disclosure submission, the OIG will begin its verification of the disclosure information. Matters uncovered during the verification process that are outside the scope of the matter disclosed to the OIG, may be treated as new matters outside the provider self-disclosure protocol.

How to disclose

In the event a provider ultimately decides to proceed with a voluntary disclosure, the following approach is recommended: The provider should share, in summary form, the following information:

- The error, and the general cause of the error, if known
- A discussion of the efforts undertaken to discern the scope of the problem(s)
- The time frame reviewed
- The estimate of the overpayment, and how it was calculated
- Any corrective action taken by the provider

How to balance the risks and benefits

The balancing of benefits and risks is complex, and should be undertaken only with advice of counsel. If the best direction is not clear, answering the following questions may help to inform the decision-making process:

First and foremost: Can you handle the situation as an ordinary matter? If providers can withdraw or amend erroneous claims prior to their adjudication by the fiscal intermediary, they can "disclose" in that way, thereby potentially avoiding the additional expense and aggravation of having the claims considered a disclosure. Usually, this option is limited to claims pending in the intermediary system.

Second: Are the circumstances and seriousness of the underlying misconduct such that a self-disclosure is likely to reduce the burden of an investigation, and thereby mitigate any penalties?

Third: What is at stake? Is someone's personal freedom at risk because of a potential jail sentence? If a federal health care program financial loss has occurred, what was the extent of such loss? Is the provider willing to repay the overpayment? If not, can the provider seek to reduce the penalties based on its ability to repay?

Fourth: has the provider had the same or similar problems with the OIG, CMS, the carrier, the intermediary, or the state? Is there evidence that the provider knew, or should have known, that his or her conduct was prohibited?

Fifth: is the provider willing to make the necessary changes in billing practices, standards of conduct, and internal control systems to ensure compliance with the law going forward?

FIGURE 6.1

MODEL DISCLOSURE LETTER TO FISCAL INTERMEDIARY AND MODEL REVIEW MECHANISM

Date: XXXX

It was a pleasure to speak with you today. This letter will memorialize the information regarding the above referenced FullSpectrum facility, a Medicare-certified CORF, in Home town, Anystate.

As we discussed, FullSpectrum recently identified an issue in certain Medicare claims. Specifically, the facility had understood that certain CPT codes for office visits could be billed by the CORF in addition to specific therapy modalities. During a limited period of time, when the UB92s were prepared for Medicare beneficiaries, the charges associated with the office visits were included under the PT revenue code. On review, we determined that the visit codes utilized were physician office codes. No physician services were rendered.

The internal audit department of FullSpectrum's parent, Big Picture, conducted a review of claims and was able to identify the amount of the erroneous claims. We have enclosed information related to our internal review and the results of that review.

As we began our internal investigation, we took the following additional steps:

1. FullSpectrum has stopped billing for physician-based CPT codes, and has not included charges related to those codes on UB92s.

FIGURE 6.1

MODEL DISCLOSURE LETTER TO FISCAL INTERMEDIARY AND MODEL REVIEW MECHANISM (CONT.)

2. FullSpectrum has ceased any collection efforts related to claims that included charges related to physician codes.

3. FullSpectrum has also arranged coding training sessions for billing office and clinical staff, to be conducted as soon as possible.

As a result of our internal review procedures, a check in the amount of _____ is enclosed. This reflects the amount of claims actually paid by Medicare on codes. It does not reflect copayment amounts. We would like your guidance on how to address the copayment issue.

If you have any questions regarding the attached materials, please do not hesitate to contact me.

Sincerely,

FIGURE
6.1

MODEL DISCLOSURE LETTER TO FISCAL INTERMEDIARY AND MODEL REVIEW MECHANISM (CONT.)

REVIEW MECHANISM:

I. GOAL OF REVIEW

The goal of the review is to identify all amounts claimed with the Medicare program that identify charges for office visits that did not accurately describe services rendered.

II. TIME PERIOD

The review period specified was May 1, 1996 - May 31, 1998. The period was identified to coincide with a policy instituted by a former business office manager to bill for office visits, through the time when the issue was identified.

III. THE REVIEW MECHANISM

FullSpectrum did not maintain computerized records adequate to identify Medicare claims that included charges for office visits.

Fortunately, FullSpectrum maintained logs of codes, billed by payor-type each month, based on CPT codes. This log is called the *Code Analysis*. We have assumed the validity of the *Code Analysis* based on the fact that it was prepared concurrently and for purposes of tracking revenue, not for purposes of this review.

Based on the *Code Analysis* log, we were able to determine with reasonable certainty the number of times office visit codes were

FIGURE 6.1

MODEL DISCLOSURE LETTER TO FISCAL INTERMEDIARY AND MODEL REVIEW MECHANISM (CONT.)

included in the calculation of Medicare patient charges. We multiplied the FullSpectrum customary charge for the CPT codes, multiplied by the frequency noted in the *Code Analysis,* to arrive at total charges.

We next reviewed the remittance advices for the relevant period to determine whether claims billed were, in fact, paid. We identified a sample of Medicare claims, and compared actual claims submitted in individual billing files, against remittance advices. In our sample, we were able to verify that payments were made.

Having satisfied ourselves that we had an accurate accounting of the number and value of claims submitted, we then multiplied the amount claimed by the ratio of costs to charges on the 1996 and 1997 cost report.

For 1998, the claims at issue had not yet been included on a cost report. Accordingly, we applied the 1997 cost-to-charge ratio to the 1998 claimed amount to arrive at the overpayment.

IV. CONCLUSION

We have concluded, based on the above review methodology, that Medicare paid FullSpectrum _____ for the office codes.

When it comes to self-disclosure, there is no single right answer for every situation. By taking into account the risks and benefits outlined in the preceding pages, hwever, the provider, through discussion with counsel, can try to steer the best course and make the appropriate decision.

1 67 Fed. Reg. 3662 (2002). CMS states this proposed rule would simply memorialize the long-standing responsibility for providers, suppliers, individuals, and other entities to report overpayments, and simply establishes the time frame and process for making those reports. CMS states its view that failure to report an overpayment within a reasonable period of time may, in certain circumstances, establish criminal liability and result in a referral to the OIG.

2 See also the Medicare rule on waiver of liability, Sec. 1879 of the SSA, which permits payments to be made for certain services and items that are not Medicare benefits where parties did not know or could not reasonably have been expected to know that services were not covered by Medicare. C.F.R. 42 C.F.R.§ 411.40 (a). This section of the SSA is refered to as the "limitation on liability" or "waiver of liability" provision.

3 "Question: What is the OIG's policy regarding the reporting of federal health care program overpayments by providers under CIAs? Answer: Providers under CIAs must promptly notify the appropriate payor of all identified overpayments and must promptly repay the overpayment amount in a manner consistent with the payor's policies." 67 Fed.Reg. 3662.

4 www.usdoj.gov/04foia/readingrooms/chcm.htm

5 Program Integrity Manual (CMS Pub.83) (PIM) §8.4.1 Procedures for the Benefit Integrity (BI) and Medical Review Units on Unsolicited/Voluntary Refund Checks.

> All Medicare contractors receive voluntary refunds (amounts received for which there was no established accounts receivable). Providers may identify overpayments through internal compliance efforts or ad hoc internal investigations. Subsequently, providers should refund such identified overpayments. Fiscal intermediaries generally receive voluntary refunds in the form of an adjustment bill, but may receive some voluntary refunds as checks, or reported as credit balances.

> Voluntary refund checks payable to the Medicare program shall not be returned regardless of the amount of the refund. Refer to PIM, Chapter 3, Section 8.4, for the acknowledgement of voluntary refunds. The contractor shall ask the provider why the voluntary refund was made, how it was identified, what sampling techniques were employed, what steps were taken to assure that the issue leading to the overpayment was corrected, the dates the corrective action was in place, claims and claims information involved in inappropriate payments, methodology used to arrive at the amount of the refund, and if a full assessment was performed to determine the entire time frame and the total amount of refund for the period during which the problem existed that caused the refund.

> When a provider returns an overpayment equal to or greater than 20% of the contractor's total annual Medicare payments for that provider (or in any other circumstances in which there are suspected patterns of inappropriate payment), the contractor shall perform data analysis for patterns of inappropriate program payment (e.g., payment for ser-

vices not rendered, payment for medically unnecessary services, or payment for upcoded services). The data analysis shall be for the period that is the subject of the voluntary refund. Conduct further medical review, if appropriate. In making that determination, consider whether the refund accurately reflects the full disclosure of the debt and that appropriate adjustments were made to the claims and the claims history files. Consider if the provider is currently the subject of a prepayment or post-payment review. Access the Fraud Investigation Database to determine if the provider is subject to any program safeguard activity. ... If fraud is suspected, immediately refer the case to the BI unit for appropriate action.

Responding to search warrants

Federal law enforcement agencies are increasingly using court-ordered search warrants for corporate workplaces and facilities to further white-collar investigations. This trend has resulted in corporations suffering the spectacle and disruption of federal agents arriving without notice on the company doorstep, search warrant in hand. Health care organizations are no longer exempt from such tactics.[1] It is helpful for providers to be proactive and to have policies in place instruct employees on who to contact and how to respond to investigators. See Figure 7.1, sample notice to employees responding to investigators, on page 124.

To protect the company's rights and interests, in-house counsel need to be prepared to react quickly and appropriately in cases where the government has chosen to execute a search warrant instead of issuing a grand jury subpoena. The following discussion and checklist will help a company's counsel prepare for and react to this disturbing law enforcement tactic.

The execution of a search warrant: Background

The use of search warrants to gather evidence of white-collar crime is a relatively new development. Before, the government would usually gather evidence of a white-collar crime by serving grand jury subpoenas for documents on companies and individuals. The company would then have a period to gather the documents and potentially narrow the scope of the subpoena. It was understood that the company would respond without destroying evidence. The government reserved its use of search warrants to crimes in which the evidence could disappear quickly, such as drug cases. A grand jury subpoena served on an occupant at a personal residence requesting the occupant to deliver, in two weeks, all illegal drugs, is not likely to be successful. Instead, the government would obtain a search warrant and, using surprise, enter the residence and search for the illegal drugs.

Companies can no longer expect to receive a grand jury subpoena in place of a search warrant. The recent emphasis on prosecuting white-collar crime has led the government to execute search warrants to obtain, quickly and comprehensively, evidence of such crimes. In short, the government will use the tactic of surprise to obtain evidence.

The government executes a search warrant without warning. Generally, the search will not be executed by one or two people in business suits, but instead by a team of agents wearing flak jackets and sidearms, who descend *en masse* upon the workplace. As described in detail below, the process is extremely disruptive to your business. If the warrant authorizes the collection of electronic information, the agents can seize the company's computers. In addition, agents will attempt to interview employees, who will likely be intimidated by the agents and who will likely not know their rights when this occurs.

To respond effectively and appropriately, your in-house counsel and compliance officers must know what to do.

What you must know about search warrants

A search warrant is a written court order issued by a federal judge or magistrate, or a judge of a state court of record with jurisdiction over your company's premises, directing a law enforcement officer to search specific premises and seize specific types of property. See Figure 7.3 on page 141. In the federal system, the warrant must be requested by a federal law enforcement officer or an attorney for the government. It must be based upon a finding that grounds for the warrant exist or that there is probable cause to believe that the grounds exist. Those grounds are usually set forth in a sealed affidavit to the court. See Rule 41 of the Federal Rules of Criminal Procedure.

Warrants must be executed within 10 days of the date they are issued, and generally must be served during the daytime, which means between the hours of 6 a.m. and 10 p.m. The agents may use force when necessary to execute the warrant. The officer taking property under the warrant is required to deliver a copy of the warrant and a receipt for the property taken. You also are entitled to an inventory of the property taken. At some point, you will be able to obtain copies of the documents seized. You also may be able to obtain a copy of the underlying search warrant affidavit from the court clerk, if the judge authorizing the warrant permits it.

FIGURE
7.1   SAMPLE NOTICE TO EMPLOYEES: RESPONDING TO INVESTIGATORS

The health care industry is one of the most highly regulated industries in the country. From time to time, the government conducts audits and investigations regarding the goods and services provided by health care organizations. As a result, certain state and federal agencies may be pursuing information and we would like you to be prepared.

Should you be approached by a representative of the state or federal government or any investigating agency regarding our company, we would ask you to please refer that individual to _____ immediately to answer any questions. Only _____ can consent to release Company information to an investigator, unless there is a search warrant. If you are presented with a search warrant, please call _____ or _____ immediately.

You are not obligated to speak to investigators. If you choose to speak with an investigator, please let _____ know in advance, if possible. You may set up an appointment to talk to the investigator at a future time. You may have legal counsel present. We will provide you with advice from legal counsel if the inquiry affects the company. Even if you do not seek counsel, we recommend that you take someone with you to any interview. You should take notes about the conversation.

If an investigator approaches you outside of the office setting, please be sure that you ask the investigator which agency he or she represents. TELL US! Get his or her business card. You should be sure to ascertain the nature of the questions they wish to ask before agreeing to discuss any matter. Should you be asked to sign any affidavit or statement, we urge you to seek legal counsel, either independently or through our company. Be sure that any document you sign fully and accurately reflects your statement and does not omit relevant facts or call for you to speculate or guess. If you have no first-hand knowledge or information relevant to the proposed statement, you should so advise the investigator.

Finally, as health care providers, we are duty bound to preserve the confidentiality of our patients' medical records. No personal health information, including documents, records, or patient information, should be provided to anyone outside the company without the express knowledge of _____ unless there is a search warrant involved.

If you have any questions, please do not hesitate to call _____
We are proud of the services rendered by our company and its employees.

What you should do when a search warrant is executed on company property?

Given the disruption that inevitably follows from the execution of a search warrant, it is important that your company get an experienced lawyer on the scene as quickly as possible. The search warrant process can take many hours, and it is not unusual for it to last the entire day. It is much better to have a lawyer present to control your company's response to the search, as well as to ensure that the agents conducting the search do not overstep their bounds. If you cannot be present, then you must monitor the government's actions by appointing someone at the facility to keep you updated as the search progresses. There is only so much that you can do by long distance, however. In any case, it is useful to get a local attorney who is familiar with search warrants to go immediately to the facility and provide some kind of assistance. Given that the process will take a long time, you must be patient and prepared to spend the whole day responding to various issues as they arise.

Initial steps

The first call you get may be from the receptionist or security guard at the front desk. You should tell that person to ask the agents to sign in at the front desk in accordance with company policy, which will create a list of the agents and their agency affiliations. In addition, ask the caller to try to get a business card from each agent. By receiving the business cards, you may be able to tell which agencies are involved in the investigation. For example, the FBI may supply the lead agent as well as others, but there may be agents of the Department of Health and Human Services (HHS) Office of Inspector General (OIG), or from the Department of Labor. This may give you a better indication of the precise nature of the investigation. It is also good to have a list of everyone present in case there are any issues that arise from the search itself. The company has a right to see the credentials of each agent par-ticipating in the search.

In addition, the company is not required to consent to the search, and you should ensure that no one at the company does so. If an agent asks for consent, the facility personnel should understand that the response should be no. This, however, does not mean that the company should deny access to the agents to conduct their search. Instead, it is merely a way to ensure that if there are legal problems with the search or the warrant, the company does not waive its rights to object.

You will also want to get a copy of the warrant as quickly as you can. If you are on the scene, get one from the agent. If you are not on the scene, have someone there get the copy and fax it to you. The agents are required to show you the search warrant. That is, after all, the legal document that permits them to conduct a nonconsensual search.

If it will take more than a few minutes for you to get there, ask to speak to the lead agent by phone. There will always be a lead agent who is ultimately responsible for how the search is conducted. In speaking with the lead agent, emphasize that the company will do everything it can to make sure the search proceeds smoothly, but that as counsel for the company, you would like them to hold off for a few minutes until you arrive. It is unlikely that the agent will agree to delay the search, especially if it will take more than a few minutes for an attorney to get to the facility. If the agents will not wait, ask if they will participate with you in a conference call to the Assistant U.S. Attorney or the Magistrate for the purpose of making the same request.

If you cannot get there within a reasonable time, do as much as you can by phone and have someone else work on getting a company lawyer or outside counsel to the scene. For companies that have several locations, it is prudent to have already contacted attorneys in proximity to each facility who can arrive at the facility quickly on an emergency basis. If you have done so, you should then call one of these attorneys and request that he or she get to the facility as quickly as possible to oversee the search. It is most helpful to have an attorney familiar with criminal law present, but any attorney who can impose some sense of order in terms of the company's response to the search, and who can also remain in contact via telephone with a lawyer with white-collar experience, is useful.

In addition to arranging for the presence of an attorney, you should also contact the most senior person at the facility to explain what is going on and outline the government's rights and the company's rights. This is likely going to be the person who will try to keep the facility running smoothly in the face of the search's disruption. Be prepared to stress to this person the necessity of remaining calm.

When you receive the warrant, you should carefully review it and take note of

(1) the exact premises to be searched

(2) exactly what is to be seized

(3) who issued the warrant

(4) any time limits for executing it

If the agents conducting the search go beyond the specified premises, the specified items to be seized, or the specified time limits, try to contact the responsible Assistant U.S. Attorney to insist upon their respecting the terms of the warrant. For example, your facility may comprise several different buildings, each with a separate address. If the warrant is limited to a particular address, which means a particular building, and the agents go to search a different building at a different address, you should first inform the lead agent that you are not granting permission for the government to search the other address, and that the agent should stop such a search. If the agent does not stop, then you should request that they hold off until you get in touch with the Assistant U.S. Attorney.

You should also contact your public affairs department as soon as you possibly can. In most cases, a search is a public event and news will leak out quickly that it is occurring. In some cases, the government has called the media before actually executing the warrant to allow the media to be present when it is executed. Your public affairs department may get calls from the press and should be advised, generally, not to comment upon or confirm anything.

Monitoring the search

The search will start when the lead agent says it will. There is nothing you can do personally to stop it. What you can do, however, is monitor it, learn from it, and possibly modify it to allow your company to continue to carry on its normal business activities. The goal of monitoring the search is to learn as much as you can, as an aid to understanding the nature of the government investigation and as a starting point for your own internal investigation.

From the lead agent, you should be able to determine who is the lead government attorney handling this matter. Often it will be the Assistant U.S. Attorney who has applied for the search warrant. You should have an attorney with white-collar experience call the government attorney and try to find out the nature of the investigation, whether the company is a target or a subject, whether any company employee is a target or a subject, and whether there is a grand jury involved. Do not panic if they will not immediately tell you. They are obligated by law to eventually tell you before any further serious legal action can be taken. The information you learn will assist you in directing the course of your internal investigation.

Be prepared to provide an office or workplace for the lead agent. You will have multiple conversations with this agent over the course of the search. Try to resolve any problems related to the search with the lead agent, as opposed to having multiple discussions with the various agents. In the end, it is the decision of the lead agent that will carry the day.

You should centralize the company's response by establishing a communications center at the facility and at your office. The search will likely raise many questions as it is executed, and therefore, you should keep the telephone lines clear for ease of communication. You should assign a senior person at the facility to monitor the search from beginning to end, and report to you at regular intervals. If issues arise, you need to address them immediately.[2]

Often, agents will split up to conduct the search. You have the right to view the search as it progresses. You should assign one person from the company to each agent or group of agents for the entire period of the search. That person should accompany the agent or agents to observe their conduct, take extensive notes regarding the places searched, the time involved in each part of the search, and the conduct of each agent.

These people are observers only, and not people who actually help the search. If the agents talk to an employee, these observers should make note of the employee's name and the substance of the conversation. These people should not offer to assist the agents in their search and they should not volunteer information. This is not to say that they cannot tell the agents where to find a restroom or where to find a certain office. Instead, the observers should not engage in substantive discussions with the agents.

During the search, it is likely that government agents will seek to interview employees. By doing so, the government seeks to obtain admissions that can be used against the company and the individual employee. Unfortunately, people who are not properly prepared for an interview (for example, by reviewing documents that can refresh their recollection) can make inaccurate or incomplete statements. Although you cannot instruct employees not to speak to the agents, you may, if circumstances permit, have a lawyer with white-collar experience advise employees that they are not obligated to speak to the agents, that they are entitled to be represented by an attorney during any interview, and that the company will provide such representation.

The search warrant does not give the government authority to conduct interviews against an individual's wishes. It is not akin to a grand jury subpoena that requires the individual's presence before the grand jury. Any interview must be consensual and may not be done by placing the individual in custody, without reading that individual his or her constitutional rights. The government agents, however, often request that employees answer questions without telling them that they have a right not to answer questions. For most people, it is difficult to refuse to answer questions that are posed by an armed agent of the United States government. Given this, some companies choose to send all the employees home so they are not available for interviews during the search, and since the workday will likely not be productive anyway.

If an employee talks with the agents, you should make note, at the earliest possible time, of his or her name and the substance of the conversation. You can then return to that employee later to get a more detailed rendition of the conversation.

The observer assigned to each agent or group of agents should observe their conduct, the places searched, the time involved in each part of the search, and the conduct of each agent. This should be in as much detail as possible. For example, the observer should note which office was searched, which files were searched, how much time was spent searching individual files, and what documents were taken. To the extent possible, the person should make an inventory of everything seized by any agent. It is also useful to have a videotape or photographs taken during the search. That way there is no doubt as to how the search was conducted.

During the search, you should ensure that the observers alert you if the agents are about to search files that may contain attorney-client privileged materials. It is not unusual for law department files or other attorney-client privileged materials to be part of the search. Guidelines in the manuals issued to U.S. Attorneys, however, provide that a search warrant should normally not be used to obtain attorney-client materials. Ask the person conducting the search to stop because of the nature of the materials involved. Once again, it is important to have an attorney with white-collar experience try to reach the Assistant U.S. Attorney handling the case, and impress upon the Assistant the seriousness of what the agents are about to do. If that lawyer cannot reach the assistant or cannot persuade the assistant to protect the material, the white-collar lawyer should contact the Magistrate who issued the warrant or, if that fails, any judge who can be reached.

It is not in the government's interest to taint its investigation by reviewing attorney-client privileged information. If agents review the privileged material, the company may be able to get a judge to order the government to drop its case or to put a Chinese wall around those agents who reviewed such materials. This is an important issue worth pressing. Often, you can work out an agreement with the Assistant U.S. Attorney so that potentially privileged material is separately boxed and sealed, and agents who are not part of the investigation will be allowed to review it for privilege at a later date.

At the conclusion of the search

Eventually the search will end. Before the agents leave the premises with any-thing they have seized, the company is entitled to receive a detailed inventory listing the items that are being seized. This inventory is made as the agents conduct their search. If you have had adequate time to instruct the people accompanying the agents, you may want them to make their own inventories of the documents and items seized by the agents. The agents may ask you to sign a receipt for the seized items. You are not required to sign such a receipt for the inventory, and you should not do so if you are asked. After all, you have no way of knowing whether the inventory accurately reflects all documents or items that were seized.

In addition, you should try to obtain copies of the documents before they are taken off the premises. You may not succeed, but ask anyway. If the agents are removing documents that are essential to carry on the business of the company (e.g., computer software or engineering drawings) you have a legitimate claim, especially if they can be easily copied on the spot without damaging the originals or impeding the search. This is an area in which you can be a bit more insistent. Remember, everyone has a boss somewhere. Do not be timid about escalating the request to a higher level of authority.

This direction is especially true of computer systems. Often the government will bring computer equipment and try to take an image of the data on your servers. Sometimes the agents are successful, sometimes they are not. If they cannot take an image, the agents may seize the computers. If those computers are essential to carry on the company's business, then you have a good argument to go all the way up to the Magistrate to try to work out an alternative solution.

At the very end of the search, you should personally escort the lead agent from the premises. Ask the agent to confirm that the inventory is a complete list of everything seized. That list may become important if you move for return of property, pursuant to Rule 41 of the Federal Rules of Criminal Procedure. You should also check with your security guards to make sure that all the agents have left the facility. Note the time the search was completed.

As soon as the agents leave, careful note should be made of all the offices and other areas searched. For each area, list the names of the people who work there. Go through the area and identify what was taken, and interview each person about the items taken. This will be very helpful in the ensuing investigations—both your own and the government's. Also, carefully inquire whether any agents spoke to any employees. If any conversation took place, gently but firmly get the specifics of that conversation from the employee.

From what you have been able to piece together, you should see the outlines of the government's focus of investigation. You should be able to identify the people in your company who know the most about those issues. From there, you will begin the process of an internal investigation as discussed earlier in this book.

Finally, reassure your fellow employees. They will be, in all likelihood, anxious and upset about the search. It is helpful sometimes to put out a short factual memo, indicating that a search occurred and that the company is working with the government to determine the focus and nature of the investigation.

What you can do to prepare for a search warrant

Before you hear the knock on your door, you should take certain steps to ensure an appropriate and smooth response. First, you should develop and appropriately disseminate a corporate policy for every facility you operate. That policy should clearly state that if any law enforcement personnel arrive, the company's lawyers should be notified immediately, before the agents are allowed onto the property. That policy should be signed by the general manager of the facility, and copies should be made available to all department managers. In addition, you should conduct special training classes to explain issues like company policy and the law relating to search warrants, service of process on company property, and requests to interview company employees. Training should include a special briefing for appropriate levels of management at the facility and corporate level.

At each facility, the guard or receptionist should have your name and number by the phone. You should also give them an alternate person to call if they cannot reach you immediately. As discussed above, if the facility is remote from your location, you should have a local attorney who knows the facility and is available on an emergency basis. In addition, each facility should have available written instructions for employees to use when accompanying agents during a search. These instructions should be very basic: e.g., get a pencil and paper, go wherever the agents go and write down what they do, say, or seize; do not answer the agents' questions; call the communications center every 20 minutes, and more frequently if something of note occurs. These instructions should be typed up and available in multiple places around the company. Often, some sort of division deskbook is a good place to keep such instructions.

You should also mark law department files and, to the extent possible, attorney-client communications as "Attorney-Client Confidential and Privileged Communications." This will at least slow the agents' efforts to seize the material. Finally, you should identify competent criminal counsel to be contacted immediately if a search warrant is executed on company property.

SERACH WARRANT CHECKLIST

1) Before the search—What you can do to prepare for a search warrant

- Develop and appropriately disseminate a corporate policy with regard to search warrants for each facility that you operate. The policy should clearly state that if any law enforcement personnel arrive, company lawyers should be notified before the agents are allowed onto the property.

- Conduct special training classes to explain the law and the company's policy relating to search warrants, service of process on company property, and requests to interview company employees.

- Ensure that the guard or receptionist at each company facility has by the telephone the names and phone numbers of the company counsel and at least one alternate contact person.

- Ensure that each company facility has written instructions in multiple locations for employees to use when accompanying agents during a search. These instructions should be very basic.

- Mark law department files and, to the extent possible, attorney-client communication as "Attorney-Client Confidential and Privileged Communications."

- Identify competent criminal or health care counsel, to be contacted immediately if a search warrant is executed on company property.

- Become familiar with your rights. For example, warrants generally must be served between the hours of 6 a.m. and 10 p.m. Also, an officer taking property under the warrant is required to deliver a copy of the warrant, an inventory, and a receipt for the property taken.

FIGURE 7.2

SEARCH WARRANT CHECKLIST (CONT.)

2) What to do when the agents arrive

- Inform personnel that execution of the search warrant can take many hours, and that they must be patient and prepared to spend the whole day with the agents. Consider sending home any unnecessary personnel.

- You are not required to consent to the search, and should not do so.

- If possible, tell the security guard to ask the agents to sign in at the front desk, thereby creating a list of the agents and their agency affiliations. Ask for a business card from each agent.

- Get to the scene as quickly as possible. If you are not an attorney experienced in these matters, have one who is accompany you or meet you there.

- If you can be on the scene within a reasonable time, but not immediately, ask to speak to the lead agent by phone. Emphasize that the company will do everything it can to make sure the search proceeds smoothly, but that as counsel for the company you would like them to hold off for a few minutes so that you can get there and make sure that everything is in order. If the agents refuse to wait, ask if they will participate with you in a conference call to the Assistant U.S. Attorney or the Magistrate for the purpose of making the same request.

- If you cannot be on the scene within a reasonable time, do as much as you can by telephone and have someone else work on getting a company lawyer or outside counsel, to the scene.

- Contact the most senior person at the facility, explain what is going on, and outline the rights of the company and the government.

FIGURE 7.2

SEARCH WARRANT CHECKLIST (CONT.)

4) Monitoring the search

- Establish a communications center at the facility and at your office. Have a senior person at the facility monitor the search from beginning to end, and report to you at regular intervals.

- Assign one person from the company to each agent or group of agents to observe their conduct, the places searched, the time involved in each part of the search, and the conduct of each agent. To the extent possible, the person should also make an inventory of everything seized by the agent.

- If possible, have the company employee take pictures while the search is being conducted.

- These observers should not offer to assist the agent, and should not volunteer information.

- If an employee talks with any agents, make note of his or her name and the substance of the conversation.

5) Protecting sensitive information

a) Confidential attorney-client information

- Guidelines in the manuals issued to U.S. Attorneys provide that a search warrant should normally not be used to obtain attorney-client materials. If the search extends to law department files or other attorney-client privileged materials, ask the person conducting the search to stop because of the nature of the materials involved.

- If the person conducting the search refuses to stop, try to reach the Assistant

FIGURE 7.2

SEARCH WARRANT CHECKLIST (CONT.)

- Contact your public affairs department as soon as you can. They may get calls from the press and should be advised, generally, not to comment upon or confirm anything.

- Identify the lead agent and the lead government attorney handling the matter. Try to resolve any problems related to the search with the lead agent, as opposed to having multiple discussions with various agents.

- Have experienced white-collar counsel ask the lead attorney and/or lead agent what the nature of the investigation is, whether the company is a target/subject, whether any company employee is a target/subject, and whether there is a grand jury involved. Do not panic if they refuse to tell you immediately; they are obligated by law to tell you eventually, and at least before any further serious legal action can be taken.

3) Ensuring compliance with the terms of the search warrant

- Get a copy of the search warrant immediately. Carefully review it and note (1) the exact premises to be searched; (2) exactly what is to be seized; (3) who issued the warrant; and (4) any time limits for executing it.

- If the agents conducting the search go beyond the premises, items, or time limits specified in the warrant, try to contact the responsible assistant U.S. attorney to insist upon their respecting the terms of the warrant.

- Government agents may seek to interview employees during the search. Although you cannot instruct employees not to speak to the agents, you may, if circumstances permit, advise employees that they are not obligated to speak to the agents, that they are entitled to be represented by an attorney during any interview, and that the company will provide such representation.

FIGURE
7.2

SEARCH WARRANT CHECKLIST (CONT.)

U.S. Attorney handling the case and impress upon him or her the seriousness of what the agents are about to do.

• If you cannot reach the Assistant or your persuasive powers have failed, contact the Magistrate who issued the warrant or, if that fails, any judge you can reach. This is an important issue worth pressing.

b) Classified and confidential information

• Privacy rules under the Health Insurance Portability and Accountability Act of 1996 (HIPAA) generally permit the disclosure of personal health information or PHI in the context of an investigator. Classified information presents special problems in the context of search warrants. Try to determine if the agents have appropriate security clearances. Contact your resident government security officer quickly, and seek guidance. If you do not have resident security officers, contact the local office of the Defense Investigative Service (DIS), or contact the customer's security representative for special access programs.

6) Bringing the search to a close

• Before the agents leave the premises with anything they have seized, obtain a detailed inventory. You are entitled to receive one, and you will probably notice that the agents are making this inventory as the search progresses. You are not required to sign a receipt for the inventory, and you should not do so if you are asked.

• Try to obtain copies of the documents before they are taken off the premises. You may not succeed, but ask anyway. Certainly, if the agents are removing documents that are essential to carry on the business of the company, you have a legitimate claim—especially if the documents can be easily copied there without damaging the originals or impeding the search. This is an area in which you can be a bit more insistent. Do not be timid about escalating the request to a higher level of authority.

FIGURE
7.2

SEARCH WARRANT CHECKLIST (CONT.)

- Personally escort the lead agent from the premises after the search. Ask the agent to confirm that the inventory is a complete list of everything seized.

- Check with your security guards to make sure that all agents have left the facility. Note the time that the search was completed.

7) What to do after the search is over

- Immediately take careful note of the offices and all other areas searched. List the names of the people who work in each area. Go through each area to identify what was taken, and interview each person about the items taken. This will be very helpful in the ensuing investigation—both your own and the government's.

- Carefully inquire whether any agents spoke to any employees. If any conversation took place, gently but firmly get the specifics of that conversation from the employee.

- From what you have been able to piece together, you should see the outlines of the government's focus. You should also identify the people in your company who know the most about those issues, in order to begin an internal investigation.

- Finally, reassure your fellow employees. They will be, in all likelihood, anxious and upset about the search.

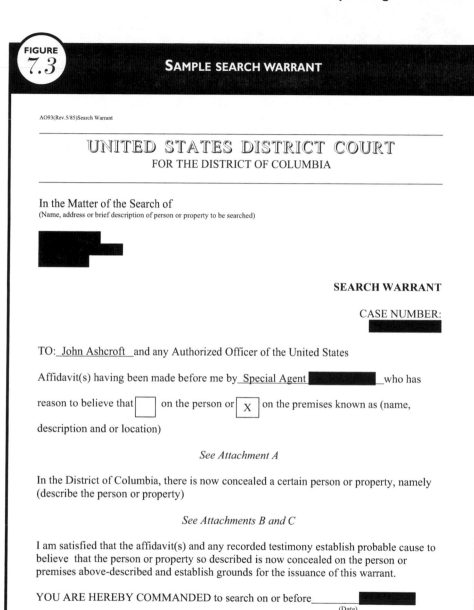

FIGURE 7.3

SAMPLE SEARCH WARRANT (CONT.)

established) and if the person or property be found there to seize same, leaving a copy of

this warrant and receipt for the person or property taken, and prepare a written inventory

of the person or property seized and promptly return this warrant to the undersigned U.S.

Judge/U.S. Magistrate Judge, as required by law.

▮▮▮▮▮▮   9:44   at Washington, D.C.

Date and Time Issued

ALAN KAY
U.S. MAGISTRATE JUDGE

_____   _____

Name and Title of Judicial Officer   Signature of Judicial Officer

[1] See, e.g., "HealthSouth Charged in Fraud," Newsday (March 20, 2003) (search executed on Health South's headquarters in Birmingham, Alabama); "Federal agents raid Tenet offices in San Diego," San Francisco Chronicle (Dec. 20, 2002) (searches executed on two administrative offices at Alvarado Hospital Medical Center); "Texas Medicaid Contractor's Records Seized Amid Allegations of Fraud and Overcharging," Health Care Fraud Report, Vol. 5, No. 5 (March 7, 2001) (searches executed at offices of National Heritage Ins. Co. in Austin and Plano, Texas); "FBI Agents Execute Search Warrants, Copy Documents at Florida Pharmacy," Health Care Fraud Report, Vol. 5, No. 18 (Sept. 19, 2001) (searches executed at Liberty Medical Supply and Liberty Medical Home Pharmacy).

[2] Classified information presents special problems in the context of search warrants. If your facility is a cleared facility, you must try to determine if the agents have appropriate security clearances. They may have some clearances, but not others. Contact your resident government security officer quickly, and seek guidance. Take careful notes of everything said or done with regard to classified documents, especially any directions given to you by the security officer. If you do not have resident security officers, contact the local office of the DIS, the federal agency responsible for security oversight for classified materials at your company, or contact the company's security representative for special access programs.

What the Sarbanes-Oxley Act means to you

Introduction

In July 2002, President Bush signed the Sarbanes-Oxley Act (SO Act) of 2002 into law in the wake of a string of accounting scandals, rapid stock market de-clines, and eroding investor confidence in the capital markets. The purpose of the SO Act was "to protect investors by improving the accuracy and reliability of corporate disclosures made pursuant to the securities laws and for other purposes."

This chapter provides a brief overview of the principal requirements of the law that apply to boards and management of publicly traded companies, with an eye towards compliance and litigation matters.[1]

The SO Act altered the prosecutorial landscape by imposing significant disclosure and corporate governance requirements on public companies and their directors and executive officers, and by dramatically increasing the exposure of companies and executives to criminal liability for white-collar offenses. Attorney General John Ashcroft hailed the new law as providing a consistent and formalized structure for corporate governance and control.

The SO Act equips the Department of Justice with new tools to hold white-collar criminals accountable and imposes tough, consistent penalties for those who would threaten the integrity of our financial markets. Among other important provisions, the act imposes new criminal penalties for securities fraud, attempts or conspiracies to commit fraud, certifying false financial statements, document destruction or tampering, and retaliating against corporate whistleblowers. The act also contains enhanced penalties for mail and wire fraud and ERISA violations.[2]

In March and April 2003, the Justice Department filed charges against nine HealthSouth Corporation executives in the first-ever enforcement of the SO Act for willful fraudulent filings.[3] Eight guilty pleas were obtained from former HealthSouth executives, including its former CFO. As of this writing, a ninth case was still pending.

The health care organization also faces recently filed charges from the Securities and Exchange Commission (SEC), difficulties from its creditors, the possibility that it will be delisted from the New York Stock Exchange, and a congressional investigation. The Justice Department's investigation is "active and ongoing and additional charges are expected to be filed."[4]

Although the law's requirements are limited to public companies, officers of any organization, including nonprofits and privately held corporations, may be affected by the SO Act's new corporate conduct standards—particularly those that restrict certain corporate activities and enhance corporate transparency.[5]

Declining bonuses, increasing lay-offs and the atmospherics created by the accounting scandals have contributed to a dramatic increase in the number of employees and former employees disclosing evidence of financial fraud. All nonpublic health care organizations should seriously consider adopting some of Sarbanes-Oxley's new rules in an effort to enhance institutional account-ability and responsibility.

The law changed the landscape for conducting business. Officers and directors of public companies, nonprofit organizations, and privately held companies are now on notice. The Justice Department now "has new tools with which to restore America's marketplace of integrity."[6] It intends to use those tools.

Enhancing corporate transparency

Several of the SO Act's provisions were specifically designed to enhance cor-porate transparency and accountability, and to instill investor confidence in corporate governance. These provisions require: 1) CEOs and CFOs to certify the accuracy of financial reports; 2) public companies to hold their senior executives to a code of ethics and encourage anonymous reporting of corpo-rate misconduct; and 3) public companies to disclose significantly more infor-mation in financial reports than previously required. The act increases the independence and authority of outside auditors and companies' audit com-mittees, and also mandates that attorneys who practice before the SEC report corporate misconduct.

CEO/CFO certification requirements

The most well-publicized requirement of the SO Act relates to CEO/CFO cer-tifications of financial reports. Sections 302 and 906 of the act require CEOs and CFOs of public companies to provide two new certificates. The require-ments in both sections underscore the importance of having internal controls to ensure compliance with a wide range of regulatory schemes to detect and prevent violations that could have a material impact on a company.

Section 302 certifications

Section 302 of the act requires CEOs and CFOs of public companies to certify, in connection with all quarterly and annual filings, the contents of the report and the company's internal controls. Specifically, CEOs and CFOs must certify that they

1) have reviewed the financial report

2) are responsible for establishing internal controls (that are different from historical internal accounting controls) that ensure discovery of material information

3) have reviewed the company's internal controls within 90 days prior to the report, and have presented their conclusions about the controls' effectiveness in the report

4) have reported all "significant deficiencies" in the company's internal control system and all fraud by persons with a role in the internal controls to the company's outside auditors and audit committee

CEOs and CFOs must also certify that the financial report: 1) does not contain materially false statements; 2) does not omit material facts necessary in order to make the statements made not misleading; and 3) fairly presents the company's financial condition and operation. The SO Act also requires a company's CEO and CFO to indicate whether or not significant changes were made to the company's internal controls, or whether there were significant changes in any other factors that could have substantively affected the company's internal controls, including any corrective actions with regard to significant deficiencies and material weaknesses.

The SEC's August 29, 2002 final rule (SEC Release No. 33-8124) indicates that the CEO/CFO certification requirement must go beyond a mere assurance that financial reports show "overall material accuracy and completeness." Although the law leaves the inner workings of the internal control process largely to the discretion of the company, the SEC recommended in its final rule that companies "create a committee with responsibility for considering the materiality of information and determining disclosure obligations on a timely basis."

Section 906 certifications

Section 906 of the SO Act creates a new CEO/CFO certification requirement in connection with all financial periodic reports that contain financial statements. CEOs and CFOs are required to certify in the 906 certificate that the periodic financial report fully complies with SEC requirements, and contains information that "fairly presents, in all material respects, the financial condition and results of operations of the issuer."

A CEO or CFO who files a 906 certificate knowing that it does not comport with the Section 906 requirements faces up to a $1 million penalty and up to 10 years incarceration, or both. An officer who *willfully* certifies a financial report knowing that it is false faces up to a $5 million penalty or up to 20 years incarceration, or both. The circumstances under which the SO Act's criminal penalties will be applied will likely be the subject of much litigation.

Code of ethics for senior financial officers

Section 406 of the act directs the SEC to adopt rules requiring public companies to disclose, along with their periodic SEC reports, whether they had adopted a code of ethics for senior financial officers. On January 23, 2003, the SEC set out the new requirements for a code of ethics for senior financial officers in a final rule (SEC Release No. 33-8177).[7]

The final rule does not require public companies to amend their existing code of ethics or even adopt a code of ethics for senior financial officers. The SO Act requires companies only to disclose in their annual report whether they have adopted a written code for senior financial officers. If a company does not amend its code of ethics to meet the SEC's criteria or does not adopt a code of ethics, it must disclose the reasons why it did not do so.

Although companies may adopt different codes of ethics for different categories of officers, directors, and employees, a code of ethics will meet the SO Act's criteria only if it has standards that are geared to detect wrongdoing, and that promote the following standards:

1) Honest and ethical behavior, including the ethical handling of actual or apparent conflicts of interest between personal and professional relationships

2) The full, fair, timely, accurate, and understandable disclosure of information in reports submitted to the SEC and in other public communications

3) Compliance with government laws, regulations, and rules

4) The prompt internal reporting of code violations to an appropriate person or persons identified in the code

5) Accountability for adherence to the code of ethics

Whistleblowers

Whistleblower protection

Although the act is primarily thought of as accounting and securities fraud legislation, it includes whistleblower provisions with accompanying civil and criminal penalties. These provisions have broad and serious implications for employers in labor, employment, and safety matters.

Although pre-existing federal law prohibited retaliation against witnesses for providing information to law enforcement relating to the commission of a federal offense, no federal law expressly prohibited retaliation against employee whistleblowers. The SO Act contains stiff civil and criminal penalties for any acts of retaliation against whistleblowers.

Criminal

Section 1107 of the act prohibits companies from taking any retaliatory action against employees who provide truthful information to a law enforcement officer "relating to the commission or possible commission of any Federal offense." Individuals who respond inappropriately may be charged with a felony offense punishable by a fine of up to $250,000 and up to 10 years' incarceration, or both. Entities may also be subject to criminal penalties under the act and fines up to $500,000.

Civil

The SO Act also contains civil penalties for unlawful retaliatory activities. Section 806 of the act prohibits public companies from terminating, demoting, suspending, threatening, harassing, or discriminating against an employee who has commenced or participated in an investigation or proceeding relating to an alleged violation of the act, any SEC rules, or any federal law relating to securities fraud, so long as the employee reasonably believed that the reported conduct violated the act or federal securities laws.[8]

Employees who are adversely treated because of protected whistleblowing activities are given the private right to sue their employer within 90 days of the date of the adverse action for "all relief necessary to make the employee whole" such as reinstatement (with the same seniority status) and back pay with interest.[9] Successful Sarbanes-Oxley plaintiffs may recover special damages such as litigation costs, expert witness fees, and reasonable attorneys' fees. They may also be entitled to "pain and suffering" damages as well.

Compliance

A health care company is not well served by viewing whistleblowers as troublemakers under the new statutory regime. Companies must train their supervisory personnel on the act's prohibitions against retaliation, so that management responds in a prudent and cautious fashion when dealing with the termination, demotion, suspension, or reassignment of employees who have engaged in protected whistleblowing activity. It is important for a company to carefully record the rationales for its actions towards all of its employees, especially those possibly involved in protected activities. Performance issues must be carefully documented.

The SO Act differs from many other statutory provisions that provide for the protection of whistleblowers in its requirement that public companies establish and implement policies and procedures to facilitate anonymous reports of corporate wrongdoing. Although Section 301 of the act does not mandate the implementation of any specific procedures, a company can establish a clear channel for open communication of questionable accounting and auditing practices by taking the following steps:

1) Developing (or revising) a code of ethics that addresses company policies regarding retaliation, and instructs employees that the company intends to comply with federal securities laws

2) Establishing a confidential reporting system (e.g., toll-free hotline) that encourages the anonymous reporting of unlawful and inappropriate activity, and publicizing the existence of this reporting system

3) Developing policies and procedures for the prompt investigation of employee complaints that rewards the filing of legitimate complaints

4) Conducting mandatory training sessions on the new/revised code of ethics for all employees, including supervisory employees and company officers, that highlight

   a) the company's anti-retaliation policy and the consequences of violating this policy
   b) the company's confidential reporting system.

Audit committee independence and autonomy

Section 301 of the act dramatically expands the role of a company's audit committee from simply monitoring accounting policies to being responsible for broader oversight of company governance. The audit committee now plays an even more integral role in a company's financial and non-financial reporting process. Audit committees are no longer making recommendations with respect to certain auditing and accounting matters—they are serving as the decision-makers. This increased responsibility demands increased diligence, availability during the course of an audit, and possible delegation of responsibilities within the audit committee. Health care companies should review their audit committee charters and foundational documents to ensure that their respective audit committees have the authority and independence that the law requires. Failure to comply with this requirement could lead to the company being delisted from national securities exchanges, and being barred from national securities associations.

Increased responsibilities and autonomy

The SO Act and the SEC's April 9, 2003, proposed rule (SEC Release No. 33-8220) focuses on three elements of the audit committee's role: 1) its independence from the company; 2) its authority to engage and oversee outside auditors; and 3) its responsibility for developing and implementing procedures for the handling of auditing disputes.

The law demands audit committee independence. It bars audit committee members from receiving "consulting, advisory, or other compensatory fee[s]" from the company, other than as a director or committee member, and from being an "affiliated person."[10] It expands the audit committee's role by requiring it to "be directly responsible for the appointment, compensation, and oversight of the work" of accounting firms. The audit committee is given authority to engage independent counsel and other advisors to ensure that it has the requisite independent advice necessary to execute its duties effectively.

The audit committee must also arbitrate auditing controversies. The act charges the committee with resolving financial reporting disagreements between management and outside auditors. The committee must also review various newly required reports and take these reports into account in connection with its oversight of financial statements, disclosures, and internal controls. Last, section 301 of the SO Act requires the audit committee to establish procedures for the handling of complaints and "confidential, anonymous submission[s] by employee[s] . . . of concerns regarding questionable accounting or auditing matters." See the previous section in this chapter on whistleblowers.

The SO Act also curtails the authority of a company's board, executives, and shareholders to retain, fire, and supervise outside auditors by requiring the auditing firm to report directly to the company's audit committee, and not management. Management no longer controls the auditor's compensation, but the company must provide appropriate auditor compensation as directed by the audit committee.

Financial expertise

Although the act provides the audit committee with increased autonomy and authority, it also requires that the committee have the requisite sophistication, experience, and knowledge base to properly discharge its duties. Section 407 of the act requires that at least one member of the audit committee qualifies as a "financial expert" (as defined by the SEC).

On January 23, 2003, the SEC issued a final rule (SEC Release No. 33-8177) regarding the presence of financial experts on audit committees of public companies. Public companies must now disclose in annual financial reports: 1) whether their audit committee has at least one member who is an "audit committee financial expert";[11] 2) whether that individual is independent of management; and 3) the name of that person. If the company does not have an "audit committee financial expert," it must disclose the reasons for not having this expert.

Auditor independence

One of the SO Act's principal goals is to strengthen accounting firms' independence. It effected this goal by imposing more rigorous standards of independence for the outside auditors of public companies through several different provisions. Section 202 of the SO Act requires that a company's audit committee provide advance approval of all audit and non-audit services that accounting firms provide to the company.[12] The audit committee must also pre-approve all non-audit services provided by accounting firms, and these approvals must be disclosed in periodic reports. Section 201 of the act also prohibits accounting firms from providing a non-exhaustive list of services[13] contemporaneous with auditing any public company. The act also provides that the Public Company Accounting Oversight Board[14] may prohibit additional non-audit services and grant exemptions on a case-by-case basis.

The SO Act also places conflict-of-interest restrictions on accounting firms. Section 206 of the act prohibits an accounting firm from auditing a public company whose CEO, controller, chief accounting executive, CFO, or "any person serving in an equivalent position" was an employee of the accounting firm within the past year. Section 203 of the act also prohibits accounting firms from conducting an audit of a public company if the coordinating or lead audit partner of the audit performed any audit services for the company during the past five years.

Enhanced disclosure requirements

The act contains several reporting requirements for public companies relating to corporate conduct, responsibilities, and governance. Public companies now must periodically disclose off-balance financial information, their usage of non-GAAP [generally accepted accounting principles] financial measures, and the effectiveness of their internal control structure and procedures for financial reporting. They must also immediately report any ownership changes and material financial changes to their financial condition and operations.

Accelerated disclosure of ownership changes

Previously, section 16 of the Securities Exchange Act of 1934 (Exchange Act) required directors, officers, and 10% shareholders of public companies to report changes in their securities ownership by the tenth day of the month after the month of the transaction. Section 403 of the SO Act applies this requirement to purchases and sales of "security-based swap agreements" and accelerates the deadline: Form 4 reports now must be filed within two business days of the transaction. An August 27, 2002 SEC final rule (SEC Release No. 34-46421) amended relevant forms to reflect the Exchange Act's new requirements. The agency also issued a final rule on May 7, 2003, to implement the SO Act's electronic filing mandate (SEC Release No. 33-8230).

By July 30, 2003, Section 16 filers will also be required to electronically file their reports with the SEC and make those reports available on Web sites by the end of the business day following the filing of the report.

Accelerated disclosure of material financial changes

Section 409 of the SO Act adds a new Section 13(l) to the Exchange Act to require public companies to disclose material changes in their financial condition and operations on a "rapid and current basis" in an understandable manner. Companies must provide a comprehensive explanation of off-balance sheet arrangements. On January 22, 2003, the SEC issued a final rule (SEC Release No. 33-8176) that requires companies to file Form 8-K reports within five business days after any public announcement or release of material, non-public financial information about completed annual or quarterly fiscal periods.

Off-balance sheet arrangements

The SO Act also requires public companies to provide significantly more information regarding off-balance sheet arrangements in periodic financial reports and public filings than previously required.

Section 401 added section 13(j) to the Exchange Act. It requires that periodic reports containing financial statements disclose all identified "material correcting adjustments" in a separately captioned subsection of the management's discussion and analysis section of their financial report. All "material off-balance sheet transactions, arrangements, obligations (including contingent obligations), and other relationships" that might have a "material current or future effect" on the company's financial health must also be disclosed. On January 27, 2003, the SEC issued a final rule (SEC Release No. 33-8182) requiring the disclosure of all off-balance sheet arrangements "that either have, or are reasonably likely to have, a current or future effect on the [company]'s financial condition, changes in financial condition, revenues or expenses, results of operations, liquidity, capital expenditures or capital resources that is material to investors." The final rule also requires companies to provide explanations of their off-balance sheet arrangements in a separate section of their disclosure documents, and to provide an overview of certain known contractual obligations in a tabular form.

Pro forma financial information

The SO Act also establishes new rules regarding the reporting of pro forma financial information. This information cannot be misleading and must be presented in a manner that "reconciles it with the financial condition and results of operations of the issuer under [GAAP]." The January 22, 2003, final rule (SEC Release No. 33-8176) requires a public company to: 1) disclose all of the non-GAAP financial measures it used in its financial calculations; and 2) reconcile those non-GAAP measures to the most directly comparable GAAP measure.

Companies and individuals who fail to comply with the final rule could be subject to an SEC enforcement action. Failure to comply with the final rule may also give rise to a violation of Section 10(b) or Rule 10b-5 of the Exchange Act.

Internal control report

The SO Act requires public companies to submit annually documentation regarding their internal control structure and procedures for financial reporting. Section 404 of the SO Act and the SEC's June 5, 2003 final rule (SEC Release No. 33-8238) require that this internal control report include a statement of management's responsibilities for implementing adequate controls and financial reporting procedures. The report must also include an assessment of: 1) the effectiveness of the company's internal control structure and procedures for financial reporting; and 2) the process by which required disclosed information is "recorded, processed, summarized and reported." Additionally, the company's public accounting firm must attest to and report on the company's assessment of its internal controls.

Code of ethics for senior financial officers

Section 406 of the act requires public companies to disclose information on their implementation of codes of ethics for senior executives. Companies are required to disclose all changes to, and waivers from, their code of ethics within five days from when such changes were implemented or waivers[15] (including implicit waivers) were granted. The name of the person who received the waiver and the date that the waiver was granted must also be reported. This information can be disclosed in a Form 8-K submission or posted on the company's Web site[16] pursuant to the SEC's January 23, 2003, final rule (SEC Release No. 33-8177).

Audit committee composition and structure

The act requires public companies to annually disclose the composition and structure of their audit committees.[17] Companies must disclose whether they have sought Section 301-related exemptions and, if so, whether these exemptions would "materially adversely affect" the ability of their respective audit committees to act independently and comply with the SO Act.

New ethical obligations for company lawyers

The SO Act establishes a reporting system for attorneys who practice before the SEC. Many attorneys will be affected by this reporting system, including in-house counsel. Those attorneys who fail to comply with the act can face civil penalties, censure, suspension, or debarment.

Section 307 of the act requires the SEC to set minimum standards of professional conduct for attorneys who appear and practice before it. The SO

Act directs the SEC to develop a rule requiring these attorneys to report: 1) "evidence of material violations" by a company of securities laws, material breaches of fiduciary duties, or similar material violations to a company's general counsel or CEO; and 2) this information to the company's audit committee (or equivalent body) if the general counsel or CEO did not take appropriate remedial actions.

On January 29, 2003, the SEC issued its final rule (SEC Release No. 33-8185) implementing Section 307.[18] The final rule details the process by which attorneys must climb the company's corporate ladder to report client misconduct.

The final rule requires attorneys who "appear and practice before the SEC"[19] to report "evidence of material violations"[20] of securities laws, breaches of fiduciary duties, and similar violations to a company's general counsel or CEO, to evaluate that individual's response, and, if that response is not appropriate, to climb the corporate ladder with the information.[21] A company's general counsel must inquire into the reported material violation and, after conducting an inquiry, must inform the reporting attorney as to his or her determination of whether a material violation has occurred, is occurring, or will occur.

The SO Act also permits, but does not require, attorneys to disclose confidential information relating to their practice before the SEC in limited circumstances. Under the final rule, an attorney may provide the SEC with confidential information (without his or her client's consent) to the extent the attorney thinks that it is reasonably necessary to achive the following goals:

1) To prevent the company from "committing a material violation that is likely to cause substantial injury to the financial interest or property of the [company] or investors"

2) To prevent the company, in an SEC investigation or proceeding, from committing perjury, suborning perjury, or committing an act "that is likely to perpetrate a fraud upon the [SEC]"

3) To rectify the consequences of a material violation by the company "that causes, or may cause, substantial injury to the financial interest or property of the [company] or investors in the furtherance of which the attorney's services were used"

The final rule did not include the most controversial provision of the SEC's November 21, 2002 proposed rule (SEC Release No. 33-8150), which related to "noisy withdrawals" (public declarations of withdrawal from legal proceedings by outside counsel who determine that clients have not timely responded to evidence of material violations). }he SEC eliminated this provision from its final rule, but it may still implement the "noisy withdrawal" rule. It proposed an alternative to "noisy withdrawal" in a January 29, 2003, companion release (SEC Release No. 33-8186), which requires withdrawal under a narrower set of circumstances than it proposed originally, and asked for comments on both proposals.

Restrictions on corporate activities

The SO Act prohibits the following two major types of corporate activity: 1) the granting of personal loans to directors and executive officers; and 2) the trading of company stock during blackout periods.

Prohibition on personal loans to directors and executive officers

Section 402 of the act prohibits public companies from extending, maintaining, renewing, or arranging credit for most types of personal loans to their directors and executive officers.[22] Although existing loans are "grandfathered" under the

SO Act, they may not be materially modified or renewed. There are some limited exceptions to the prohibition—including certain types of business loans[23]
provided in the ordinary course of business whose terms are no more favorable
than the terms offered to the public. In addition, certain loans made or maintained by an insured depository institution are exempted under the act.
Companies must now analyze whether split-dollar life insurance programs,
company-assisted cashless stock option exercises, cash advances against future
bonuses, advances of amounts covered by indemnification, and any other programs that involve extending credit to company directors and executive
officers are prohibited by the SO Act.

Pension fund blackout periods

On January 22, 2003, the SO Act's prohibition on insider trading during pension fund blackouts became effective with the SEC's release of a final rule
(SEC Release No. 34-46778) implementing Section 306 of the act. That statutory section bars directors and executive officers of public companies from
trading company stock that was acquired in connection with their employment at times when at least 50% of pension fund participants are precluded
from doing so ("blackout period"). Under the act, a company or shareholder
can sue for the recovery of profits that were realized as a result of a prohibited sale during the blackout period, irrespective of the director's or officer's
intent. Public companies must also provide their directors and executive officers (who are subject to the trading prohibitions) with a timely notice of
blackout periods.

Forfeiture of CEO/CFO incentive compensation

The act contains executive compensation "clawback" provisions. Under section
304, if a company has to restate its financial statements because of "material
noncompliance" with financial reporting requirements, its CEO and CFO will
be required to forfeit all bonuses and incentive or equity-based compensation,

and all profits from any sales of company securities during the 12-month period following the first public issuance of the financials being restated.

Improper influence on audits

Section 303 of the act prohibits any director or officer of a public company
(or any persons working under their direction) from fraudulently influencing,
coercing, manipulating, or misleading the accountants doing audits for the
company with the intent of rendering the financial statements materially misleading. The SEC's May 20, 2003 proposed rule (SEC Release No. 34-47890)
implementing Section 303 would prevent such persons from "pressur[ing] an
auditor to limit the scope of the audit, to issue an unqualified report on the
financial statements when such a report would be unwarranted, to not object
to an inappropriate accounting treatment, or not to withdraw an issued opinion on the issuer's financial statements." Under the SO Act, the SEC may also
bring a civil lawsuit against persons who improperly influence company audits.

Penalties and enforcement

The SO Act imposes new criminal and civil penalties for fraudulent activities,
including securities fraud.

Criminal penalties and enforcement

The act increases the criminal penalties for violations of the mail and wire
fraud statutes, violations of the Employee Retirement Income Security Act of
1974 (ERISA), and the Exchange Act. It also creates new criminal penalties for
securities fraud, and clarifies the handling of penalties for attempts and conspiracies to commit criminal fraud.

Mail and wire fraud

Prior to the SO Act, the maximum period of incarceration for mail and wire fraud (18 U.S.C. § 1341, 1343) was five years, except for schemes to defraud financial institutions, which allowed for incarceration for up to 30 years. Section 903 of the act increased the maximum period for both kinds of fraud to 20 years. Section 807 of the act added 18 U.S.C. § 1348, which expanded the federal mail fraud statute by making it a crime to defraud any person, or to fraudulently obtain money or property in connection with any public company's stock.

Securities fraud

The SO Act adds new criminal penalties for defrauding shareholders of a public company. Persons convicted of securities fraud or attempted securities fraud will be subject to a fine and up to 25 years incarceration, or both.

Obstruction of justice

Sarbanes-Oxley adds two new obstruction-of-justice provisions to the federal criminal code. These provisions establish broad prohibitions against concealing documents and records in an official proceeding, and are not limited to proceedings involving securities.

Section 1102 of the act amends 18 U.S.C. § 1512 by creating a new tampering statute. An individual who "alters, destroys, mutilates, or conceals a record, document, or other object," or who attempts to do so in order to impede an official proceeding, faces a fine and up to 20 years' incarceration, or both.

Section 802 of the act creates 18 U.S.C. §§ 1519 and 1520. 18 U.S.C. § 1519 imposes fines, up to 20 years incarceration, or both, for individuals who knowingly alter, destroy, or falsify documents or tangible objects with the intent of impeding, obstructing, or influencing a federal investigation or "any matter within the jurisdiction of any department or agency of the United States." 18 U.S.C. § 1520 relates to the destruction of corporate audit records by accountants. Violators of that section are subject to a fine and up to 10 years' incarceration, or both.

Health care companies should also be mindful of two of the SO Act's provisions that assist and protect corporate whistleblowers (which are discussed on pages 134 to 137) when they are implementing policies to address obstruction concerns. Section 1107 of the act creates a new felony for persons who knowingly retaliate against persons who provide truthful information relating to the commission of any federal offense. Section 806 also creates a private right of action for whistleblowers who were retaliated against for protected activity. Violating any of these four provisions can lead to serious corporate and individual liability.

Attempts and conspiracies

Section 902 of the SO Act adds 18 U.S.C. § 1349. This section clarifies that persons who attempt or conspire to commit criminal fraud are subject to the same penalties that they would be subject to had the attempt or conspiracy been successful.

ERISA

Sarbanes-Oxley enhances the criminal penalties for violations of ERISA. Section 904 of the act amends 29 U.S.C. § 1131 by increasing the maximum term of incarceration for violators of ERISA's reporting and disclosure provisions (29 U.S.C. §§ 1021-1031) from a maximum of one year to a maximum term of 10 years. The act also increases the maximum fines for ERISA reporting and disclosure violations from $5,000 to $100,000 for an individual, and from $100,000 to $500,000 for organizations. An ERISA violator is now subject to a fine that is the greater of: 1) $250,000; 2) twice the defendant's gross pecuniary gain; or 3) twice the victim's gross pecuniary loss. Corporate violators may face a fine that is the greater of: 1) $500,0000; 2) twice the defendant's gross pecuniary gain; or 3) twice the victim's gross pecuniary loss.

The Securities Exchange Act of 1934

The Exchange Act previously provided for a maximum criminal fine of $1,000,000 and up to 10 years' incarceration, or both, for individuals, and a maximum fine of $2,500,000 for corporate violators. The SO Act increases the maximum criminal fine for individuals to $5,000,000 and increases the maximum criminal fine for corporate defendants to $25,000,000.

Sentencing for white-collar criminals

The SO Act also led to tougher sentencing standards for corporate fraud and white-collar fraud offenses. On April 18, 2003, the United States Sentencing Commission announced that it had voted unanimously to increase penalties significantly for corporate and other serious white-collar frauds. The decision, which made permanent the commission's January 25, 2003 emergency amendment, increased the base penalties for wire and mail fraud. Additionally, it expanded the scope of sentencing enhancement that targets officers and directors of publicly traded corporations to apply also to registered brokers, dealers, and other investment advisors who defraud investors or employers. It also significantly increased the penalties for individuals who obstruct justice through document destruction.

The new changes will take effect on November 1, 2003, following a 180-day period of congressional review.

Civil enforcement

Sarbanes-Oxley contains several provisions that directly increase the risk of civil liability under the securities laws, and create new kinds of civil claims for fraudulent activity.

Expanded statute of limitations for securities fraud

The litigation-related provision of the Act that has attracted the most attention lengthens the statute of limitations for private securities litigation. Prior to the

SO Act, the statute of limitations for a securities fraud action was one year from the date of discovery of the violation, or three years after the violation occurred. Section 804 of the act extends the statute of limitations for private actions alleging "fraud, deceit, manipulation, or contrivance" in violation of the federal securities laws to two years after discovery of the violation, or five years after the violation occurred, whichever is earlier.

Nondischargeable bankruptcy debts

The SO Act's bankruptcy provision will also assist securities plaintiffs. Section 803 of the act amends federal bankruptcy laws to prohibit public companies from being permitted to discharge any order or settlement from a securities-related action in bankruptcy.

Disgorgement

The SO Act establishes a fund for victims of securities laws violations and provides for a mechanism by which to reimburse defrauded investors from fines paid by corporate wrongdoers. All SEC civil penalties that a public company pays are directed to a disgorgement fund for the benefit of its harmed investors.

Officer and director bars

The SO Act strengthens the SEC's ability to remove officers and directors of public companies from their positions and to bar them from occupying similar offices at other public companies for violations of the antifraud provisions of the federal securities laws. Section 305 of the act modified the standards governing such actions by lowering the threshold of proof for obtaining an officer and director bar—the agency can now have an individual removed or barred by a demonstration of the individual's "unfitness." Previously, a showing of "substantial unfitness" was required. Under Section 1105 of the SO Act, the SEC may also prohibit violators of Section 10(b) or Rule 10(b)(5) of the Exchange Act from being an officer or director of a public company.

Freezing assets

In addition to new and enhanced criminal penalties, Section 1103 of the act grants the SEC the authority to obtain court orders freezing "extraordinary payments" from public companies that appear to be designated for "directors, officers, partners, controlling persons, agents or employees" of that company.

Practical recommendations for compliance with Sarbanes-Oxley

The Sarbanes-Oxley Act ushered in a new era of corporate responsibility. General counsels and compliance officers of public health care companies must now meet compliance and internal control issues relating to disclosure, board independence, auditing, ethics, and compliance. Boards of directors of public companies must be well versed in financial literacy, corporate governance, and accountability, as well as crisis management.

Superficial compliance with the act is not acceptable, and indeed, may work to a company's detriment. Companies that delay compliance with Sarbanes-Oxley may find themselves embroiled in criminal or civil litigation that will affect their public image and financial welfare. Forward-thinking companies that develop policies and procedures that incorporate their philosophy and operating style, principles of accountability and integrity with the letter and spirit of the SO Act will avert such troubles and achieve higher levels of corporate excellence.

Protected whistleblowing activity

The Sarbanes-Oxley Act requires companies to establish and implement policies and procedures to facilitate anonymous reports of corporate wrongdoing. Establishing and maintaining an effective confidential reporting system can not only alert a company of wrongdoing before the conduct escalates, but may also serve as a built-in defense if an anti-retaliatory claim is filed or a government investigation is initiated.

Employees must be provided a risk-free way to report wrongdoing within their internal chain of command, as well as an effective anonymous means by which to bypass their employer's internal structure in order to report management wrongdoing. The confidential reporting system must be well-publicized through signs, brochures, posters, and other forms of communication. This confidential reporting mechanism should really be operated only by an outside entity; information is more likely to get lost or be ignored with internal reporting mechanisms. Once a complaint is received, prompt and reasonable action should be taken. Only a limited number of company personnel should be involved.

Health care companies must review a broad range of employment documents to avoid interfering with protected whistleblowing reporting activity. Companies need to revise their releases, settlements, confidentiality and employment agreements, codes of conduct, policies regarding communications with regulatory and law enforcement agencies, policies relating to the reporting of corporate wrongdoing, policies related to the protection of confidential information, and all other pertinent information to ensure that these documents do not prohibit conduct protected by the SO Act.[24]

The act requires health care companies to respond prudently and cautiously when dealing with employees who have engaged in protected whistleblowing activity. Companies must be deliberative in their dealings with employees who have: 1) provided information or assisted in an investigation involving possible violations of law; 2) filed or participated in a proceeding related to an alleged violation of the law; or 3) provided truthful information to a law enforcement officer related to the possible commission of a federal offense. These employees may still be protected by the SO Act even if they were wrong about corporate misconduct and no violation actually occurred. Similarly, supervisory employees must be trained about the act's anti-retaliation provisions, as well as the civil and criminal consequences of running afoul of its anti-retaliation and witness-tampering provisions.

Ethical obligations for in-house lawyers

The SO Act imposes stringent ethics obligations on lawyers. All lawyers, including in-house counsel, must now report questionable conduct and climb the corporate ladder with their concerns until they are satisfied that the company takes appropriate remedial action. Attorneys who become aware of credible evidence of questionable conduct must report this information to their supervisors, who must then determine whether the evidence constitutes "credible evidence of a material violation." If the supervisor concludes so, they must report this information to their superior.

The general counsel or compliance officer of a health care company must be responsible for the development and implementation of well-conceived and efficient policies and procedures for the handling of attorney complaints. At the outset, a policy must be developed regarding the handling of communications between in-house and outside counsel on disclosure issues. A determination must be made regarding whether the costs and delays of the attorney-reporting ritual requires the establishment of a qualified legal compliance committee (QLCC) to handle these complaints. Establishing a QLCC (especially if an existing company committee satisfies the minimum independence required for a QLCC) would, in all likelihood, prevent duplication of efforts, and excessive bureaucracy.

Attorney training is a key component of an effective program. Companies must educate their legal staff who practice in SEC-related areas about the SO Act's requirements and procedures for handling suspected disclosure concerns. These attorneys should be trained on their obligations under the act, their right to disclose confidential information to the SEC under limited circumstances, how the SO Act defines "evidence of a material violation," and on when they must report this evidence. Proper training will help prevent reports based on ill-conceived or ill-informed observations and beliefs. This will, in turn, conserve company resources and avoid unnecessary government intrusion.

The development of internal controls

Sarbanes-Oxley places great emphasis on a company's internal controls to detect and prevent corporate wrongdoing. It requires public companies to develop internal controls to ensure: 1) the validity of CEO/CFO certifications of financial reports; 2) the independence, financial expertise, and autonomy of the audit committee; and 3) the independence of the accounting firms that they utilize. Internal controls help secure a company's compliance with the SO Act's numerous financial and non-financial disclosure requirements and restrictions on corporate activities.

Developing customized internal controls to ensure compliance with the act is a multi-step process. At the outset, a company is well advised to: 1) assess the strengths and weaknesses of its internal financial controls systems; 2) take an inventory of its existing resources, processes, and technologies; and 3) designate a small group of knowledgeable individuals to be responsible for coordinating the development of internal controls. Once this initial assessment has been made, the company must then remedy existing policies or create new ones. All policies and procedures must be based on objectivity, transparency, accountability, and compliance with applicable laws and regulations. All processes must also be well documented.

Once internal controls have been implemented and adequately documented, a company must then remain ever vigilant and self-evaluative. Employees must be made aware of their respective responsibilities relating to the company's internal controls. A selected group of management employees must continuously evaluate the company's internal controls to determine whether the controls: 1) are rigorous enough to manage the company's risks; 2) are sufficiently documented for subsequent internal and external review; and 3) adequately capture organizational changes. These evaluations must be properly documented, and the company must address all internal control deficiencies in a timely fashion.

---

[1] *The SO Act also addresses the regulation of public accounting firms, and the operations of the SEC. These issues are not covered in this manual.*

[2] *Atty. Gen. Field Guidance on 2002 Sarbanes-Oxley Act (August 1, 2002).*

[3] *See Press Release U.S. Atty's Office, N. Dist. of Ala., "William T. Owens: Health CFO Charged in Massive Accounting Fraud" (March 26, 2003).*

[4] *Id.*

[5] *For example, the Sentencing Commission's draft amendments to the United States Sentencing Guidelines questioned whether the new sentencing provisions should be applied "to cases in which an officer . . . of a large, non-public organization violates any provision of security [sic] law." See 67 Fed. Reg. 70,999, 71,000, 71,002 (2002).*

[6] *Attorney General John Ashcroft, Speech at WorldCom Conference (Aug. 1, 2002).*

[7] *The final rule applies this provision to the principal executive officer, principal financial officer, principal accounting officer and controller (and persons performing similar functions) of all public companies.*

[8] *This provision applies only to the furnishing of information to: 1) a federal regulatory or law enforcement agency; 2) a member or committee of Congress; or 3) "a person with supervisory authority over the employee (or such other person working for the employer who has the authority to investigate, discover, or terminate misconduct)."*

[9] *The employee must make a prima facie showing that his or her protected conduct was a contributing factor in the employer's retaliatory actions. The burden then shifts to the employer, who must demonstrate, by clear and convincing evidence, that it would have taken the adverse employment action irrespective of the employee's protected activity.*

[10] Determining whether an audit committee member is an "affiliated person" requires a case-by-case analysis of that member's relationship to the company and the amount of control exercised by that member. The rule provides a safe harbor in which an audit committee member who is not an executive officer, director or 10% or more shareholder of the company is deemed not to be an "affiliated person." The SEC may also grant exemptions to the "affiliated person" prohibition on a case-by-case basis.

[11] An "audit committee financial expert" must have: 1) an understanding of GAAP; 2) an ability to assess the general application of GAAP in connection with the accounting for estimates, accruals, and reserves; 3) experience preparing, auditing, analyzing, or evaluating complex financial statements or experience supervising persons engaged in such activities; 4) an understanding of internal controls and procedures for financial reporting; and 5) an understanding of audit committee functions. These attributes must have been acquired through: 1) education and experience as a principal financial or accounting officer, public accountant, or auditor, or a position involving the performance of similar functions; 2) experience "actively supervising" a person in such a position; 3) experience overseeing or assessing the preparation, auditing, or evaluation of financial statements, or 4) "other relevant experience." If the "audit committee financial expert" is qualified by virtue of having "other relevant experience," the company must describe that experience.

[12] All audit and non-audit services contracted for May 6, 2003 or later must be pre-approved by the audit committee or entered into pursuant to pre-approval policies established by the audit committee. The pre-approval policies may not allow the delegation of the audit committee's responsibilities to management. No prior approval is required for de minimis services.

[13] Namely, bookkeeping services and services related to accounting records and financial statements, financial information systems design and implementation services, appraisal or valuation services, fairness opinions or in-kind report services, actuarial services, internal audit outsourcing services, management functions or human resource services, broker, dealer, investment advisor, or investment banking services, legal services, and expert services unrelated to the audit.

[14] The SO Act called for the creation of the Public Company Accountability Oversight Board, a nonprofit entity responsible for overseeing the auditing of public companies by public accounting firms. The board, which is funded by fees from public companies and public accounting firms, may impose penalties on public accounting firms that violate federal securities laws.

[15] The rule defines "waiver" as any company approval of a material departure from a provision of the code. An "implicit waiver" is defined as a company's failure to take action within a reasonable time frame regarding a material departure from a provision of the code that has been made known to an executive officer.

[16] A company can only post this information on its website if it gives its investors advance notice of its Internet address and intention to disclose changes in or waivers to its code of ethics on its Web site. A company that discloses information in this manner must keep this information on its Web site for at least one year, and retain this information for five years.

[17] This is in addition to the existing requirement that such information be disclosed in proxy statements or instructional statements at certain shareholder meetings.

[18] The new regulations become effective August 25, 2003.

[19] The act did not define the phrase "practice before the SEC." The SEC's final rule definition includes attorneys who: 1) transact any business with the SEC, including communications in any form; 2) represent a company in an SEC proceeding or investigation; 3) provide advice on federal securities laws regarding documents that they know will be filed with the SEC; and 4) advise companies as to whether information, statements, or opinions must be filed with the SEC. The SO Act does not

apply to attorneys who conduct these activities outside of the attorney-client relationship. It does not apply to attorneys who are retained to assert a "colorable defense" in SEC investigations and proceedings in situations where the company's general counsel provides "reasonable and timely reports on the progress and outcome of [the] proceeding to the [company]'s board of directors." Investigating attorneys also have no reporting obligations if they: 1) are retained to investigate evidence of a material violation; 2) report the investigation's results to the company's general counsel; and 3) the general counsel passes this information on to the board of directors (or equivalent body).

[20] *The SEC's final rule defines a "material violation" as "a material violation of an applicable United States federal or state securities law, a material breach of a fiduciary duty arising under United States federal or state law, or a similar violation of any United States federal or state law." This definition may also incorporate decisional law concepts of materiality.*

[21] *Companies may alternatively establish a committee of outside directors ("Qualified Legal Compliance Committee") to receive attorney reports.*

[22] *The act does not define the term "executive officer." Rather, the definition of executive officer that the SEC adopted in Rule 3b-7 is applicable. Consequently, any person who is identified by a company in its annual report on Form 10-K as an executive officer is covered by this prohibition.*

[23] *The act does not automatically prohibit 1) certain extensions of credit related to home improvements; 2) manufactured home loans; and 3) extensions of credit by certain brokers and dealers.*

[24] *For example, documents and policies should be reviewed to determine if they restrict employees from communicating with or assisting in a government investigation, or participating in government proceedings. Such restrictions are commonly found in non-disclosure and non-disparagement clauses, and in covenants not to sue. These restrictions should be revised so that they do not prevent or impede protected conduct.*

Ethical considerations in conducting internal investigations—Focus on exempt organizations[1]

Ethical obligations in representing any client

This section briefly discusses the general ethical duties that should be taken into consideration when conducting an internal investigation. The same standards of professional conduct that govern all lawyers apply with equal force to attorneys representing exempt organizations. Of course, counsel representing exempt organizations should have added sensitivity to issues such as cost, avoidance of duplicative work, and ensuring that the work done is in the entity's best interest.

In representing clients, lawyers must abide by various ethical duties. The primary sources of these duties are the American Law Institute's Restatement (Third) of the Law Governing Lawyers and the American Bar Association (ABA) Model Rules of Professional Conduct, which set forth the general ethical rules. Most states have promulgated the cognates of these rules in their rules of professional conduct. Those rules are usually adopted by the bar association of the state or the court of highest jurisdiction in that state.

In addition to the rules of professional conduct that govern the lawyers in each jurisdiction, lawyers must be aware of other potential sources of duties that may govern their conduct in particular matters. For example, in matters that involve a court proceeding, the rules of that court may impose additional duties. In matters that involve a trust as a client, the rules of a probate court may govern counsel's actions with respect to a trust organized under the laws of that particular jurisdiction. For in-house counsel, the employee handbook or policies of the particular organization may impose still other duties. Counsel should not be caught unaware of the specific ethical duties that may apply to particular investigations.

Restatement (Third) of Law Governing Lawyers

Section 16 of the Restatement lays out a lawyer's general duties to a client. It provides that, to the extent consistent with a lawyer's other duties, a lawyer must, in matters within the scope of representation,

(1) proceed in a manner reasonably calculated to advance a client's lawful objectives, as defined by the client after consultation

(2) act with reasonable competence and diligence

(3) comply with obligations concerning the client's confidences and property, avoid impermissible conflicting interests, deal honestly with the client, and not employ advantages arising from the client-lawyer relationship in a manner adverse to the client

(4) fulfill valid contractual obligations to the client

Counsel also has the duty to inform and consult with a client. In particular, according to the Restatement § 20 (2000),

(1) A lawyer must keep a client reasonably informed about the matter and must consult with a client to a reasonable extent concerning decisions to be made by the lawyer

(2) A lawyer must promptly comply with a client's reasonable requests for information

(3) A lawyer must notify a client of decisions to be made by the client and must explain a matter to the extent reasonably necessary to permit the client to make informed decisions regarding the representation

Counsel should not lose sight of the fact that the internal investigation has to be performed in accordance with these general duties.

ABA model rules

The Rules of Professional Conduct contain provisions that discuss an attorney's duty to disclose a client's wrongful conduct. These rules will help guide an attorney who finds wrongful conduct as the result of an internal investigation.[2] Counsel must also consider whether there is a legal duty to disclose evidence of wrongdoing, and specifically consider whether Sarbanes-Oxley imposes any up-the-chain reporting duty.[3]

Duties to the client

At the most basic level, a lawyer has a duty to provide competent representation, which requires "the legal knowledge, skill, thoroughness, and preparation reasonably necessary for the representation." Model Rules of Professional Conduct R. 1.1 (2001) (ABA Model Rule). The rules also says a lawyer must act with "reasonable diligence and promptness" when representing a client. ABA Model Rule 1.3.

Competent representation requires that lawyers keep the client reasonably informed and comply with reasonable requests for information. Because decisions ultimately rest with the client, counsel must explain matters to the client "to the extent reasonably necessary to permit the client to make informed decisions regarding the representation." ABA Model Rule 1.4(b). As can be seen, these rules are similar to the general rules in the Restatement set forth above.

At all times, counsel must exercise independent professional judgment and render candid advice. The commentary to ABA Model Rule 2.1 explains that a "client is entitled to straightforward advice expressing the lawyer's honest assessment" and that "a lawyer should not be deterred from giving candid advice by the prospect that the advice will be unpalatable to the client." ABA Model Rule 2.1, cmt. 1. This is perhaps one of the most important rules to remember. The client is entitled to the lawyer's honest assessment, not what the lawyer believes the client wants to hear. The results of internal investigations may sometimes appear to be troubling to executives of the organization. The lawyer must give the executives his or her straightforward advice as to what appropriate steps should next be taken.

A lawyer may run across certain facts or rumors and must decide whether to recommend conducting an internal investigation or whether to raise those facts or rumors to others in the organization. In general, lawyers are not required to give advice unless asked to do so by the client. Thus, outside counsel may not have any duty to advise the client as to facts or rumors that are outside the scope of representation. Attorneys can, however, be held liable for failing to advise the client on matters within the scope of representation. The commentary to the ABA rules explains that a lawyer is not expected to give advice until asked by the client. Nevertheless, when counsel knows that the client proposes a course of action that is likely to result in substantial adverse legal consequences to the client, ABA Model Rule 1.4 may obligate counsel to act "if the client's course of action is related to the representation." ABA Model Rule 2.1, cmt. 5.

In-house counsel generally have the same obligations as outside counsel. In-house counsel, however, have a broader scope of representation, and therefore are responsible for advising the client on a broader range of issues. Whereas an outside counsel is typically hired for specific tasks, in-house counsel are charged with an entity's day-to-day legal affairs. In addition to responsibilities that all attorneys owe their clients, in-house counsel often also are bound by employee handbooks and the like, which set forth responsibilities for all employees of the entity.

It is universally recognized that lawyers have a duty to maintain client confidences. Indeed, a "lawyer shall not reveal information relating to representation of a client unless the client consents after consultation, except for disclosures that are impliedly authorized in order to carry out the representation." ABA Model Rule 1.6(a).

Notwithstanding confidentiality and the general duty to advise the client, counsel must not counsel or assist criminal or fraudulent conduct. Of course, it is perfectly acceptable—indeed, expected—to discuss the legal consequences of any proposed action with a client. The lawyer's role as an advocate demands that, in appropriate circumstances, the lawyer "assist a client to make a good faith effort to determine the validity, scope, meaning or application of the law." ABA Model Rule 1.2(d). The commentary to ABA Model Rule 1.2 further states that the provision requires a lawyer "to give an honest opinion about the actual consequences that appear likely to result from a client's conduct." ABA Model Rule 1.2, cmt. 6.

Duties to others

Despite counsel's allegiances to the client, counsel has an overriding duty of honesty and candor when dealing with third parties, particularly courts. The Rules make clear that counsel must not "knowingly" make false statements of material fact or law to the tribunal or offer evidence the lawyer knows to be false. ABA Model Rule 3.3. The commentary specifies that "an assertion purporting to be on the lawyer's own knowledge ... may properly be made only when the lawyer knows the assertion is true or believes it to be true on the basis of a reasonably diligent inquiry." Courts apply an objective reasonableness standard to determine whether the lawyer believed the representations were true. *See, e.g., Office of Disciplinary Council v. Price,* 732 A.2d 599, 604 (Pa. 1999). The same duty of honesty applies to third persons generally as it does when dealing with tribunals. See ABA Model Rule 4.1.

Organization as client

ABA Model Rule 1.13(a) makes it clear that a lawyer employed or retained by an organization represents the *organization* acting through its duly authorized constituents. As discussed in Chapters Four and Five, when interviewing employees, it is necessary to establish who the client is and to whom the attorney-client privilege belongs. Because the company is the client, the attorney must understand his or her ethical duties with regard to an organizational client. For public companies, Sarbanes-Oxley imposes specific duties.

In the context of a tax-exempt organization, the fact that the organization is the client can raise particularly tough issues. For example, if the IRS challenges the tax-exempt status of an organization based on the wrongdoing of its officers or directors, it may be in the best interests of the organization to argue that the proper sanction is not for the IRS to revoke the organization's tax-exempt status, but to impose "intermediate sanctions" personally on the wrongdoers. When those wrongdoers are the trustees of the trust or chief executives of an exempt organization, counsel must always remember his or her ethical duties to the organizational client, and not to specific individuals.

The following section discusses the general ethical objections in reporting wrongdoing. It also discusses certain concerns when representing a trust.

Reporting wrongdoing

No doubt, like most rules, the duty of confidentiality is not absolute. The ABA Model Rules make this abundantly clear: A lawyer may disclose client confidences to the extent the lawyer reasonably believes necessary

> (1) to prevent the client from committing a criminal act that the lawyer believes is likely to result in imminent death or substantial bodily harm; or (2) to establish a claim or defense on behalf of the lawyer in a controversy between the lawyer and the client, to establish a defense to a criminal charge or civil claim against the lawyer based upon conduct in which the client was involved, or to respond to allegations in any proceeding concerning the lawyer's representation of the client.

ABA Model Rule 1.6(b) and ABA Model Rule 1.13(b) offer more specific guidance to lawyers who represent organizations and other entities:

A lawyer for an organization may know that an officer, employee, or other person associated with the organization is acting or intends to act in a manner that violates that individual's legal obligation. Another possibility is that this individual is again acting or intending to act in a manner resulting in a violation of the law, and that that violation could be imputed to the organization.

A third possibility is that the individual sees someone else acting in a way that could harm the organization, and does nothing about it. In any of these situations, the lawyer should proceed as is reasonably necessary in the best interest of the organization.

In determining how to proceed, counsel can consider factors such as the seriousness of the violation, the apparent motivation underlying the conduct, the involved person's responsibility within the organization, the attorney's scope of representation, the organization's policies, and any other relevant matters. ABA Model Rule 1.13 suggests appropriate action including asking the client to reconsider, advising of the need for a separate legal opinion, and referring the matter to the highest authority that can act on the organization's behalf. If the lawyer reports a potential violation of law that is likely to result in substantial injury to the organization to the highest authority within the organization, but the highest authority insists on taking an action in violation of law (or failing to act), the lawyer may resign in accordance with ABA Model Rule 1.16.

Restatement § 96 is substantially similar to Model Rule 1.13. Section 96 makes clear that counsel representing an organization "represents the interests of the organization as defined by its responsible agents acting pursuant to the organization's decision-making procedures." It further provides that counsel must follow the instructions "given by persons authorized so to act on behalf of the organization." The provision then reiterates the procedures that attorneys representing an organization must follow when someone within the organization acts inappropriately. Restatement § 96(1).

Restatement § 73 addresses the attorney-client privilege when the client is an organization. The attorney-client privilege here extends to communications that are otherwise privileged. Those communications must take place between an agent of the organization and a "privileged person." This phrase can mean "the client (including a prospective client), the client's lawyer, agents of either who facilitate communications between them, and agents of the lawyer who facilitate the representation." The communication must concern a matter of interest to the organization. The communication can be disclosed only to "privileged persons" and other agents of the organization "who reasonably need to

know of the communication in order to act for the organization."
Restatement §§ 70, 73.

Application of the above principles when representing a trust

Who is the client?

In the trust context, it is especially important to understand precisely whom you represent. Counsel's attorney-client relationship is a bond with the trustees, who act collectively to represent the trust. A trust is not a recognized entity under the law, but instead is a relationship of obligation imposed on the trustees for the benefit of the beneficiaries of this organization. Trustees act on the this organization's behalf. In their official capacity, trustees are empowered to employ outside counsel and other service providers. Thus, outside counsel and other providers servicing the trust represent the trustees, in their collective and representative capacity as trustees.

Counsel must make no mistake: You do not represent the beneficiaries of the trust. Counsel may nevertheless owe a limited duty to beneficiaries. Although a trust attorney has an attorney-client relationship only with the fiduciary trustees and not the beneficiaries, the attorney might be obliged to notify the beneficiaries of trustee misconduct that threatens the beneficiaries' interest.[4]

In addition to the usual rules governing all lawyers, trust law imposes several special rules and obligations. Fundamentally, counsel representing a trust cannot give legal advice if the work can in no way benefit the organization. Still, as in most other contexts, the lawyer need not question the client's (i.e., the trustees'), decisions. In short, counsel may assume that trustee decisions are proper. However, trust attorneys should not assume those decision are proper if they know them to be illegal, if they are based on counsel's own negligent advice, or if they are completely adverse to the trust's interest and lacking any legitimate justification. (In-house counsel may have additional obligations as an employee to more closely monitor the decisions of trustees.)

Attorneys, similarly, are not obligated to second-guess the trustees' request for legal advice. The trustees ask for advice in order to decide on the appropriate course of action. A lawyer therefore should provide advice, even when the advice is that a specific action cannot be taken. Bear in mind, however, the usual caveat: a lawyer cannot give legal advice when the work requested can in no way benefit the trust.

In addition to the general rules that may mandate reporting of wrongdoing, there may be state rules that apply specifically to trusts.[5] The fiduciary exception to Restatement § 73 may also require disclosure to beneficiaries in certain circumstances. If you are representing a trust, you should ensure that you have reviewed all applicable state regulations and court rules.

[1] *The authors wish to thank Emmett Lewis and Shane Hamilton of Miller & Chevalier for their contributions to this chapter.*

[2] *The rules help define the standard of care that an attorney owes a client, but they do not themselves establish a cause of action. Thus, a violation of the Rules can help support a finding that the attorney violated the applicable standard of care, making the attorney liable in a malpractice action.*

[3] *See Chapter Eight for a discussion of Sarbanes-Oxley. Note, however, that Sarbanes-Oxley applies to publicly-traded companies and therefore would not apply directly to exempt organizations. Exempt organizations usually have attorneys who are IRS practitioners and who are subject to the rules governing practice before the IRS contained in what is referred to as "Circular 230." See generally 31 C.F.R. Part 10. These rules contain specific duties, including the duty in some circumstances to furnish information to the IRS; the obligation to notify a client of noncompliance, errors, or omissions; and certain due diligence requirements.*

[4] *See, e.g., Hawaii Probate Rule 42(b) (attorney representing a trust "shall owe a duty to notify such beneficiaries . . . of activities of the fiduciary actually known by the attorney to be illegal that threaten the security of the assets under administration or the interests of the beneficiaries").*

[5] *See, e.g., id. 42(b)*

Related Products
From HCPro

Audioconferences

07/24/2003 - *Internal Investigations: Know the Risks, Reap the Benefits*

The Office of Inspector General's (OIG) Compliance Program Guidance for Hospitals says that conducting internal investigations is an impo rtant part of an effective compliance program. However, the OIG does not tell organizations how to conduct internal investigations.

How critical an issue are internal investigations? Over four hundred of your peers responded to a 2003 survey on this topic for HCPro's talk group, "Compliance Talk." Seventy-five percent of the respondents said that they had been involved in an internal investigation. They also told us their most common problems include: not knowing how to define or limit the scope of an investigation, finding the resources to do it, and getting cooperation from management and staff.

Join HCPro for the 90-minute live audioconference, Internal Investigations: Know the Risks, Reap the Benefits and gain tools and strategies to conduct efficient, effective, and beneficial internal investigations and self-audits.

Why you should listen to this audioconference

This basic-to-intermediate program will show you how to run your own internal investigations from start to finish, making it a cost-effective compliance solution!

Our expert speakers are health care attorneys with significant experience in conducting internal investigation. They'll teach you best pratices for document reviews, employee interviews, compliance versus privilege issues, and avoiding pitfalls while conducting internal investigations and audits.

More specifically, Internal Investigations will show you how to:

* Recognize the need for an internal investigation
* Balance competing rights and interests among employees, directors, officers, and other constituents
* Organize and conduct an internal investigation that will protect attorney-client privilege
* Interview employees during internal investigations
* Evaluate results of an internal investigation

* Avoid pitfalls and mines in the process of internal investigations
* Manage the impact of the Sarbanes-Oxley Law

The end of the program will feature a live question-and-answer session. Bring your questions!

FEATURED SPEAKERS:

• **Mark A. Srere, JD**, is a partner in the Litigation Practice at Morgan, Lewis, and Bockius in Washington, D.C. Mr. Srere counsels corporate clients on compliance issues and internal investigations. He is involved at every stage in the representation of clients that are targets of criminal prosecution, from grand jury appearances to trials. Mr. Srere has represented companies and individuals in SEC investigations, environmental investigations, Department of Transportation proceedings, and major fraud investigations, including tax fraud. He has also represented clients involved in independent counsel investigations, including the Smaltz investigation of former Agriculture Secretary Mike Espy and the Starr investigation of President Clinton. Mr. Srere teaches "International White Collar Crime" as an adjunct professor at Georgetown University Law Center.

• **David L. Douglass, Esq.,** is a partner in the Washington, D.C. office of Porter Wright Morris & Arthur LLP, where his practice encompasses complex litigation and representing clients with respect to governmental compliance, investigations and enforcement actions. A large portion of his practice is devoted to representing healthcare providers and insurers in fraud and abuse cases.

Sign up today for *Internal Investigations: Know the Risks, Reap the Benefits* and gain tools and strategies to conduct efficient, effective, and beneficial internal investigations and self-audits.

To obtain additional information, to order the above product, or to comment on *See for Yourself: A Health Care Provider's Guide to Conducting Internal Investigations and Audits* please contact us at:

HCPro, P.O. Box 1168, Marblehead, MA 01945
Toll-free telephone: 800/650-6787
Toll-free fax: 800/639-8511
E-mail: customerservice@hcpro.com
Internet: www.hcmarketplace.com
